THREE-DIMENSIONAL
WET FELTING
felting on a ball

THREE-DIMENSIONAL
WET FELTING
felting on a ball

Natasha Smart

✳ THE CROWOOD PRESS

CONTENTS

INTRODUCTION

ello and welcome to this deep dive into the exciting world of felting on a ball! If you've not heard of this technique before, this is a method of wet felting using a ball as a mould to create 3D, hollow shapes in felt. It's an innovative way of achieving structure and depth to elevate your finished felt from flat, 2D pieces to functional and decorative 3D items which are seamless and strong enough to hold their shape.

If you've read my first book, *Wet Felting*, which includes a chapter on felting on a ball, you might wonder what's new or what else there is to say about this technique. Well, since then I've been exploring all aspects of using a ball in wet felting. I've experimented with different wool fibre breeds and embellishment materials, tested different-sized balls and fibre coverage of the balls, and expanded the felt out from them with the addition of extra structural items like handles and flaps. I've also adapted the technique itself to find better ways of achieving the best results. From all of this I've developed a range of new projects to make on the ball.

In terms of process, this book follows a logical progression, building from simple layouts utilising the rounded shape of the balls in the first main project chapter through to the addition of extra felted parts like handles, pockets and flaps in the second. We then move on to changing and expanding the surface of the felt through nuno felting on a ball with fabric, before finishing with how to approach your own projects with the inclusion of some different surface design techniques. If you're new to felting on a ball, I would recommend starting the process from the Embellished Bowl Sample Project in Chapter 2 before moving on to more challenging layouts.

The projects are illustrated with step-by-step photographs, which will help you to keep track of all the felting on a ball stages, and I've included lots of tips throughout to help you navigate successfully through them. There are also some useful extra wet felting techniques, such as instructions on how to make felted straps and cords. If you're a neat freak like me, I hope you'll also enjoy the chapter on how to give your felted items a great finish, including demonstrations of how to install zips and clasps, and tips on caring for your finished felt.

Although this book is structurally about felting on a ball, the materials and decorative surface design techniques used are just as applicable to flat felting or felting with 2D flat resist shapes, so I hope you'll be able to use these in your wet felting more generally. They are also adaptable and interchangeable between the projects I've included, so I would encourage you to tweak the designs, swap around techniques and incorporate your own ideas about what makes you excited creatively. If, from my own exploration of felting on a ball shared in this book, I'm able to give you some inspiration and confidence to try new techniques in your own felting, then that's a great outcome for me too. But whether you decide to follow one of the projects completely, or just use it to spark off an idea of your own, that's really only the start, then it's over to you to experiment with your own colours and designs.

I would love to see what you make as a result of reading this book, so please do tag me in on your creations on social media @natashasmarttextiles.

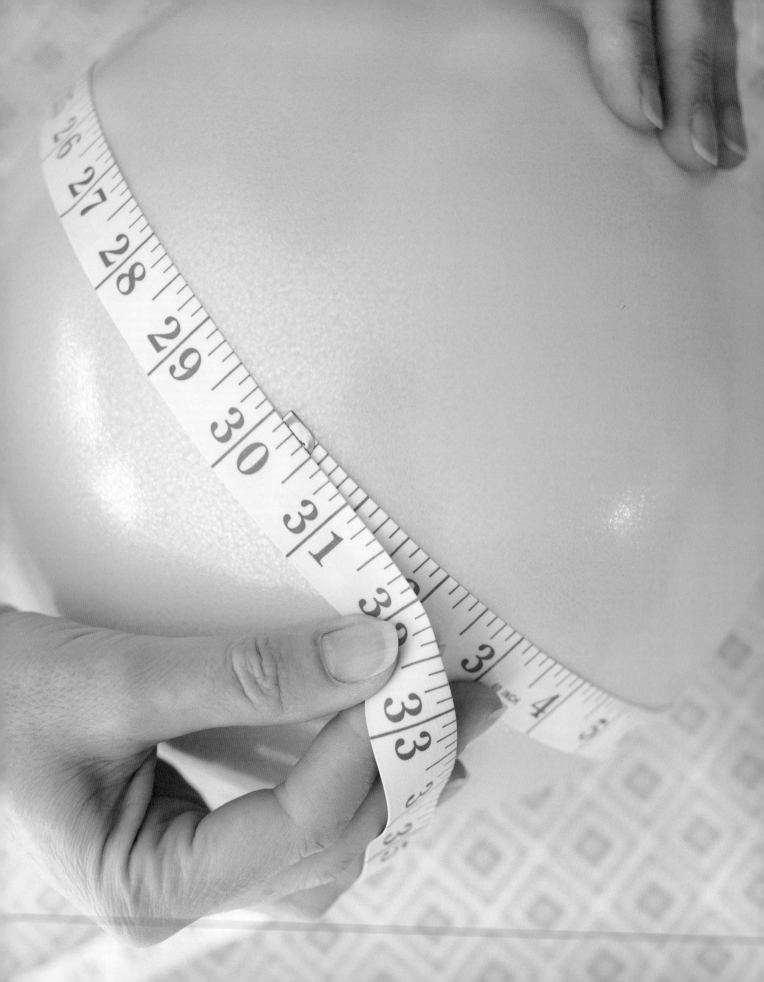

CHAPTER 1

EQUIPMENT AND MATERIALS

As this book is all about wet felting on a ball, it makes sense to start off by introducing you to a felting ball, along with the other types of ball we can repurpose for this process. So in this chapter we'll consider what a felting ball is, how we work with them in wet felting and how to prepare them with useful guidelines. We'll then look at the other equipment we need for the felting process, as well as materials.

WHAT IS A FELTING BALL?

A felting ball is a round, 3D shape which provides three key functions in felting on a ball:

- Firstly, it acts as a mould or forma to create a spherical 3D shape in felt. By placing wool fibre around the ball we can create a replica of the ball shape in felt.
- Secondly, it acts as a resist to create a hollow form with 'sides' which won't felt together. The ball literally resists or prevents the wool fibre from bonding together wherever the ball is placed in between areas of fibre.
- Thirdly, the ball provides the means to agitate the wool fibre (which is a key stage in the wet felting process) by us being able to push around and bounce the ball when it is covered by fibre.

Any type of ball will work as a felting ball, but ones which will provide the smoothest wet felting experience are made of lightweight rubber, inflate and deflate easily using a plug at the top, and will stretch to be firm and useable at a range of sizes. You can, of course, use other 3D shapes to felt around too, such as a cardboard or plastic box, but they won't have the advantage of being bounceable or offering flexibility or 'give' to the surface like a ball.

As the size range of any ball still has its limits, I've used four different balls within this book to create differently sized projects, from a small vessel to a large cat cave. Two of the balls are purpose-made felting balls, manufactured by Living Felt in Texas, USA and covering the most useful mid-range sizes, and the others are a small children's toy ball and an adult exercise ball. The main ball I've used throughout this book is the original large purple (or pink, if you've got much older ones like I have) felting ball. It's the perfect size for a range of items, like decently sized bags, hats and baskets, so it would be the one I'd recommend most.

Measuring the circumference size around the middle is the easiest way of establishing and comparing ball sizes.

Here are the approximate circumference size ranges of the four balls demonstrated in this book:

Ball colour	Blue	Green	Purple	Yellow
Size description	Small	Medium	Large	Extra Large
Circumference size range (approximate minimum to maximum)	40–53cm (16–21in)	63–76cm (25–30in)	76–94cm (30–37in)	112–122cm (44–48in)

Note that the size ranges are all approximate, due to variance between the balls, so yours may differ slightly.

Small blue children's toy basketball with marked guidelines, inflated to 51cm (20in).

Medium green Living Felt felting ball with marked guidelines, inflated to 76cm (30in).

Large purple Living Felt felting ball with marked guidelines, inflated to 86.5cm (34in).

Extra large yellow exercise ball with marked guidelines, inflated to 117cm (46in).

You don't have to use the same balls as these, however, and once you start felting on a ball you'll start spotting all sorts of items that might work: I've repurposed rugby balls and other children's toy balls equally successfully. Here are the main features of an ideal felting ball to look out for:

- Made of durable rubber, so is thick enough to firmly hold its shape, to withstand being pushed and bounced around and to be reusable.
- Made of stretchy material, so is firm enough to use at a range of sizes (most rubber balls seem to offer a circumference variance of 10–15cm/4–6in).
- Surface made of slightly tacky or textured rubber, as opposed to completely smooth, which helps the wool fibre and materials grip to it more successfully.
- Bounceable, which is important for the felting on a ball technique and is why I wouldn't recommend balloons (good stretch but not hardy or bounceable) or beach balls (hardy but no stretch and not bounceable).

- Inflates and deflates via an easily removable top plug, as opposed to a valve, which requires a specific pump attachment.

It's worth noting that, although felting balls are sold by their circumference range size, most other balls tend to be sold by height, which makes finding the right size a little confusing. Luckily there's a very simple mathematical formula to help you work out the circumference size from the height or diameter: height or diameter × 3.14 (pi) = circumference. For example, the small blue children's mini basketball I use is classed as '16cm' (6.25in) in height, which correctly equates to approximately 50cm (19.75in) in circumference using this formula.

Obviously the felting ball's most important function is as a starting size mould/resist to create the felt around, but it can also provide a useful function as a finishing size forma for shaping the finished felt. If you re-inflate the ball inside your wet, finished felt it will stretch it into a rounded shape, smoothing out surface wrinkles and holding the shape whilst the felt dries. Rubber balls which are firm at a range of sizes are useful for this, as the felt will be smaller by the end so the same ball you used to create the felt can simply be re-inflated at a smaller size to shape it. (NB: It's also possible to use differently shaped finishing formas than just round/spherical, which I cover later in this chapter.)

INFLATING YOUR FELTING BALL

The felting balls come with a top plug which is easy to use – just avoid holding your inflated ball by the plug as there's a risk of pulling it out! They also come with a straw to inflate them by blowing into it. It is possible to inflate the balls in this way, but I would recommend using some kind of pump (hand, bicycle, foot, for example). There needs to be some kind of nozzle at the end of your pump to insert into the plug hole, but this doesn't need to be a perfect fit. The hole is large enough for you to just hold a nozzle in place at the opening whilst you inflate it.

The other type of balls are the ones like a football which have a valve opening (such as the small blue ball). To inflate or deflate the ball you need a special valve attachment for your pump, which usually comes either with the ball or with the pump. When the valve is removed the air stays inside the ball. This style is useful for felting in that there is no plug sticking out, however I've found that, with a lot of use, the valve starts to leak air so longevity might become an issue.

CARING FOR YOUR FELTING BALL

It's also worth briefly looking at how to care for your felting ball. There are a few aspects to this:

- Inflating size. One of the great features of a rubber ball is that it is firm enough to use at a range of sizes. However, this means that when you are inflating a ball, it doesn't simply stop at the ideal or manufacturer's advised size, it will keep going. Be aware that you might be pushing the ball beyond its limits by continuing to inflate it. This happened to me when I over-inflated a ball to use as a finishing forma overnight and returned the next day to find it had burst. I would therefore recommend avoiding inflating too far beyond the sizes set out in the table earlier in this chapter (you can generally tell when a ball is going beyond its capacity because it loses its flexibility and becomes hard), and use the same ball as both your starting and finishing size forma within the same project.
- Avoid using sharp objects near the ball. Save all of your amending (with scissors, sewing needle or a felting needle) until prefelt stage when you have removed the ball.
- Cleaning and storage. After use, and once you've deflated it, re-insert the top plug and give it a quick wipe with a dry towel. I tend to leave mine to air dry for an hour or two before putting them away, storing them out of direct sunlight.

Felting balls laid flat, along with a rechargeable electric pump with nozzle attached, plastic straw, top plug and metal valve attachment.

MARKING GUIDELINES ON THE FELTING BALL

Although you don't need guidelines on the ball for a simple project, such as a bowl, it helps to have an idea where the top, sides and bottom of the ball are so that you can plan where your embellishment materials and wool fibre colours will end up on your finished item and how big your top opening will be. And with more complex structural projects, such as the Backpack Project in Chapter 4, it becomes more crucial to use set markings to ensure all the elements are felted in the right place. I've therefore developed some useful guidelines to mark on the ball which will help you plan and structure your projects.

As an example, let's mark up the large purple ball, which is the main ball used in the projects in this book. The steps below show you how to create the markings and include a brief explanation of how you can use each one. I'll then show you equivalent measurements, where relevant, for some of the other balls.

MARKING UP THE LARGE FELTING BALL

WHAT YOU WILL NEED

Equipment
- Large purple felting ball
- Inflating pump
- 25cm (10in) internal diameter round bowl or similar to prop up the ball
- Tape measure
- Permanent marker pen

Step by Step

Step 1: Marking the top circle line

Inflate the ball to a circumference of 86.5cm (34in). To create the top circle line, which denotes the standard top edge for fibre layout for items such as bowls and bags, measure 8cm (3.25in) out from the centre of the plug. Measure and mark points all around the ball and then draw in the line to create a circle.

Step 2: Marking the top placement lines

Measure and draw lines to divide the top circle into four equal quarter segments. Divide each quarter segment in half again with a dotted line. Assign and mark each segment with a letter sequentially from A–D, so that A and C (and B and D) are opposite. These markings help to keep track of the front and back of the item you're making and provide equal placement for structural elements such as side tabs for a bag.

Step 3: Marking the top edge line

To mark the top edge line, which designates the top fibre layout line for projects with a wider opening, such as baskets, measure 12cm (4.75in) out from the centre of the plug. Measure and mark points all around the ball and then draw in the line.

Step 4: Marking the middle design line

To mark the middle design line, which denotes the centre of the main design area visible on your finished item, measure 21.5cm (8.5in) out from the centre of the plug. Measure and mark points all around the ball and then draw in the line.

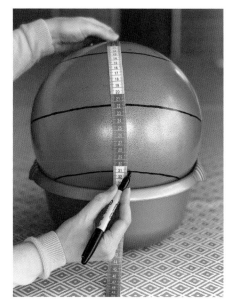

Step 5: Marking the base edge line

To mark the base edge line, which designates the typical base edge for projects on the ball with a base or flat bottom, measure 31cm (12.25in) out from the centre of the plug. Measure and mark points all around the ball and then draw in the line.

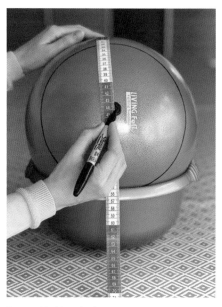

Step 6: Marking the base centre point

To mark the very bottom point of the ball, which is useful for creating surface designs emanating from the base of the finished item, such as a spiral, measure 43.5cm (17in) out from the centre of the plug. Measure and mark points going right around the ball and draw a small circle to mark this point approximately.

The table below shows the equivalent guideline markings I used for the four balls in this book. Here are some final points to note about the measurements shown:

- I marked up the balls at different circumference sizes (at the most common sizes for the projects, hence I've included two sets of sizes for the large purple ball), so the measurements are different for marking the guidelines on each one, however the proportions are the same. So if you were able to inflate all the balls to the same size once marked, which of course you can't, because each ball has its own size range and limitations, you'd find that the guidelines are all in the same place. The exception to this is the top circle line on the yellow ball, which I created specifically for the Cat Cave Project to give a smaller opening hole.
- I haven't included some of the markings on the blue ball, as it is so small, or the yellow ball, as I did not need them.
- The measurements will work for any ball, as long as you inflate your ball to the circumference size shown.

- I always measure out from the centre of the plug or opening hole.
- Don't worry if your measurements are slightly out (up to 1cm/0.5in) as that's a size tolerance that won't make any difference to your finished items.
- Avoid following the ball manufacturing lines around the middle to mark your middle design line as they aren't always reliable, although the blue ball helpfully already had an accurate middle design line marked by the basketball lines printed on it.
- I've rounded some of the measurements up or down slightly for simplicity.
- Bear in mind that all these sizes denote the starting size for the felt which, after shrinkage, is likely to be approximately 25 per cent smaller.

Ball colour	Blue (Small)	Green (Medium)	Purple (Large)	Purple (Large)	Yellow (Extra Large)
Circumference size	51cm (20in)	76cm (30in)	86.5cm (34in)	91.5cm (36in)	117cm (46in)
Top circle line	5cm (2in)	7cm (2.75in)	8cm (3.25in)	9cm (3.5in)	9cm (3.5in)
Top edge line	N/A	11cm (4.25in)	12cm (4.75in)	14cm (5.5in)	N/A
Middle design line	12.5cm (5in)	19cm (7.5in)	21.5cm (8.5in)	23cm (9in)	29cm (11.5in)
Base edge line	N/A	27cm (10.5in)	31cm (12.25in)	33cm (13in)	N/A
Base centre point	25cm (10in)	38cm (15in)	43.5cm (17in)	46cm (18in)	58.5cm (23in)

OTHER TOOLS AND EQUIPMENT

Apart from the felting ball, most of the other tools and equipment you'll need are non-specialist items, some of which you may already have around your home. Here are the main items, along with a brief description of each and how you use them.

Measuring Tools

Measuring scales are essential for weighing out fibre, to ensure the right thickness and structure in the finished projects, and for ensuring consistent results.

Typical wet felting equipment you'll need for felting on a ball.

Digital measuring scales for weighing wool fibre.

Bowls

I use several different-sized bowls for any felting on a ball project, each with a separate purpose:

- A bowl smaller than the ball size, to use to prop the ball up in as you work.
- A bowl just larger than the ball size (when covered with fibre), to complete the push rub stage of the process within (*see* Chapter 2). This should ideally be a relatively snug fit so that you're not having to move the ball around within it a lot for the ball to make contact with the sides of the bowl, but you should still be able to move it easily.
- A large bowl of any size to hold the soapy water solution.

Selection of plastic, china and glass bowls, along with a large plastic tub.

Although the propping-up bowl should ideally be round, the other bowls could be round or square. If you use bowls at different sizes it might be worth getting a few options. I mainly use Wham Casa brand bowls at the following approximate diameter sizes (NB: These bowls are sold based on their external measurements, but I have used the internal measurements throughout this book for comparison with whatever bowls you may have):

External Bowl Diameter	Maximum Internal Bowl Diameter and Height	Maximum Ball Circumference Size
28cm (11in) diameter round bowl	25cm × 12cm (10in × 4.75in)	70cm (27.5in)
32cm (12.5in) diameter round or square bowl	28cm × 14xm (11in × 5.5in)	86.5cm (34in)
36cm (14in) diameter round bowl	32cm × 15cm (12.5in × 6in)	91.5cm (36in)

To use the extra large yellow exercise ball, or similar, you will need a large tub of some kind (or use the bath!) to accommodate it. With the yellow ball inflated to 117cm (46in) in circumference I found that a 40-litre tub was a good size (actual external measurement 43cm/17in in diameter × 32.5cm/12.75in high).

Tights/Pantyhose

Tights or pantyhose, with the legs cut off, are a simple way of covering the wool fibre once we've completed the layout, to keep the fibre in place and protect it during agitation. Tights also give us something to hold onto to facilitate bouncing. I use a range of sizes with different balls, but if you just aim for a large-sized pair it will be fine for most projects. You'll need two pairs of each for complete coverage, apart from when using the small blue ball, when one pair will be enough.

I use Pretty Polly Smooth Knit brand, which are 20 denier so very stretchy (the XXL size fits over the large 40-litre tub) and not too delicate, and they can be reused repeatedly:

- Small/medium (86–102cm/34–40in hips)
- Medium/large (102–122cm/40–48in hips)
- XXL (137–152cm/54–60in hips)

Prepared tights/pantyhose in small/medium, medium/large and XXL sizes.

Bubble wrap is a handy work surface to use for creating flat felt pieces, such as the flap and strap in the Backpack Project and the prefelt in the Jurassic Basket Project. It's a bit too bulky to wrap around the ball but if you need to keep elements from felting together you could use it as a resist, as well as a packing material to help shape the finished felt. I tend to use bubble wrap with small bubbles and always have the smooth side next to the fibre, on the basis that this will cause least disruption to any design.

Soap

I like to use washing-up/dishwashing liquid in my soapy water solutions as it's fully soluble, and I prefer to use solid olive oil soap for hands-on rubbing. I often use it from prefelt stage, on elements such as the inside embellishments and handles, as it adds a concentrated amount of soap to the felt which helps your hands rub the surface more smoothly.

Spray Bottle/Ball Brause (or Brauser)

During the embellishment and fibre layout I use a spray bottle to add extra soapy water, which has a gentle spray so there is less danger of everything sliding off than from the concentrated shower of a ball brause. Once I remove the ball, however, and the fibre has bonded to prefelt stage so won't be disrupted, then the ball brause comes into its own for me by delivering a much heftier shower of soapy water.

To use the ball brause, make up your liquid soap solution in a separate container, dip the end of the bulb into it, squeeze and release. The bulb will draw up the water which can then be sprayed over the work through the shower head.

To prepare the tights, turn them inside out so that the seam lines aren't against the ball when you use them, and tie a knot in each leg approximately 7.5cm (3in) down from the gusset centre join. Cut off the leg excess. Keep the legs when you cut them off, as they come in useful for making straps (*see* the Backpack Project in Chapter 4) or for covering very small balls.

To get the tights onto the ball, I stretch them over a large bowl first and then place the ball inside, lifting up the tights around the ball and being careful not to drag them across the fibre. Gently pull them up as far as they will go, which will probably leave the top of the ball exposed. Repeat the process with a second pair of tights, placing the ball inside so that the area not covered by the first pair is now covered. You don't need to tie or knot the tights at the top, keeping them loose is fine and avoids having to continually untie them.

Thin Plastic/Bubble Wrap

Wrapping the fibre in a thin sheet of plastic before putting on the tights helps to keep the fibre in place, helps to keep water next to the fibre and stops the fibre from felting to the tights. I use a roll of DIY/builder's polythene sheeting, which is thin but holds up well and can be reused, but you could repurpose large plastic bags or similar. Any thin plastic which will mould around the fibre and isn't too bulky would be ideal. A 100cm × 55cm (40in × 22in) piece would work for most projects (except the larger Cat Cave Project).

Using the ball brause to give a concentrated shower of soapy water.

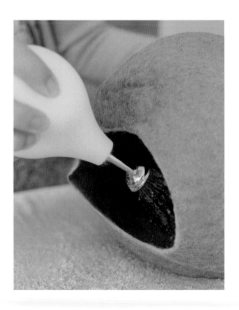

Using the Mini Wedge Palm Washboard to rub the edges of a felt strap.

Rubbing Tools

When making flat felt, it is helpful to use some kind of rubbing tool to agitate the surface more quickly than your hand alone. There are a range of handmade wooden Palm Washboard tools made in the USA by HeartFelt Silks which work really well for this.

Another option with agitating the fibre is to rub the felt against something like a textured mat or drawer liner. This is particularly useful for final shaping of the felt.

Towels and Trays

As we're dealing with so much water during the felting on a ball process, having plenty of towels to hand is useful: as a work surface, for mopping up water and for towel drying the finished felt. Another useful option to help contain dripping water from the ball and bowls is to stand them in a shallow tray such as a boot tray.

Resist Templates

Foam resist templates used for several of the felting on a ball projects.

1mm and 6mm foam resist templates.

Tools for making paper templates.

Typical items which can be used or repurposed as finishing formas or shapes.

Some of the projects in this book incorporate additional flat resist templates to create hollow areas within the felt, such as pockets in the Dartmoor Basket Bag and Backpack Projects and the ear shapes for the Cat Cave Project. Thin foam or plastic is ideal to use for these: thin foam is better for inserting between layers, as it's flexible, mouldable and not too bulky; for an external element which needs to be more substantial and rigid, like the ear shapes, then a thicker 5–6mm foam (sold as Ethafoam) is perfect. You'll also want paper (graph or squared paper is useful), ruler for measuring, pens/pencil for marking (including a permanent marker pen for marking up the felting ball) and household scissors for cutting out shapes.

Finishing Formas

Felting balls can also be used as finishing formas to shape the finished felt and stretch the surface smooth, along with other 3D items. A hat block is an example of a purpose-made forma to shape and stretch a hat around (although you don't need to use one for the hat projects in this book), but you can easily repurpose household items such as plastic and cardboard boxes, tins and bowls.

Finishing and Other Tools

Other tools which are essential for felting on a ball include sewing scissors of different sizes and a tape measure for measuring and marking up the felting ball. There are also some specific tools/materials required for completing some of the projects, such as: crochet hook, pompom maker, clothes pegs, textile glue, screwdriver, seam ripper, packing tape, sewing needle and pins. Felting needles are handy for joining wool fibre, and a steam iron and pilling tool (to remove wool pills) are useful for finishing the surface of your felt.

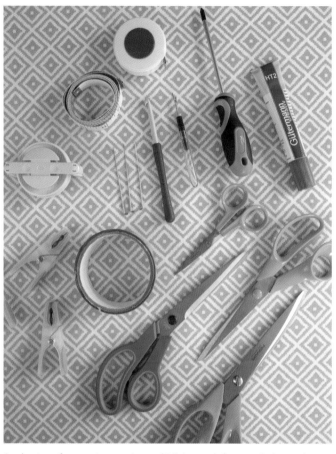

A selection of measuring, cutting and joining tools for completing projects.

A steam iron and pilling tool are useful for creating a smooth finished felt.

MATERIALS

Wool Fibre

Wool is the common term for the natural hair or fibres that form the fleece of animals, in particular sheep. Sheep's wool has unique properties which enable us to matt the fibres together to make felt (which we'll cover in the next chapter). Once you start delving into it, you'll find that wool is a vast subject, covering different animals (such as sheep, goats and alpacas), different breeds (such as Merino, Corriedale and Shetland sheep) and different forms (such as batts and tops, rolags and locks, yarns). There is a confusing amount of terminology, which differs for different countries. In this section, and based on my own understanding, my aim is therefore to simplify what is available and what will work well for felting on a ball, focused on the sheep's wool fibre and other materials used in this book.

Comparing wool fibre

There are hundreds of sheep breeds, all with different wool characteristics and, from a feltmaking perspective, suitable for different end results. Some, like Merino, produce a very fine fibre, which is perfect for creating items where softness, fineness and drapability are all desired, such as garments to be worn next to the skin. Most others produce a coarser fibre of

The sheep breed fibres used in this book are all largely similar in terms of microns (apart from Merino), as they represent the slightly coarser and more hardwearing felted items shown in the projects. Here are their approximate micron details, for comparison (and you'll see that fibres of the same breed can vary in thickness, depending on the supplier):

Breed	Microns
Merino	19
MC-1 (USA sheep)	25
Finnwool	26
Corriedale (combed tops)	26.5
Maori/New Zealand	27
Kent Romney	27-29
Maori-Bergschaf	27–33
Shetland	29–31
Corriedale (sliver)	29–30
Bergschaf	30–33

varying thicknesses, which works well when you are looking for a thicker, sturdier felt which has good weight and will hold its structure. So there is a lot out there to choose from. To help us navigate through all this, different sheep breed fibres are categorised by the thickness of each individual fibre strand using microns: one micron = one millionth of a metre (or one thousandth of a millimetre). The smaller or lower the micron count, the finer the fibre. This is the most consistent method of measurement used worldwide, which will enable you to compare fibres from different breeds and suppliers.

Preparing wool fibre

Wool fibre is generally processed into three main forms commercially for feltmaking (using UK terminology):

- **Carded batt**, in which all the individual fibres are intermingled and laid out in fluffy, lofty sheets.
- **Carded sliver**, which is like carded batt but processed into a long, narrow tube.
- **Combed top/tops**, which are also processed into long tubes, but the individual fibres are combed in one direction to make them smoother, sleeker and uniform.

To use wool fibre in wet felting, the first stage is to take the commercially prepared fibre and divide it into manageable pieces or wisps, which we then lay out and layer up together to construct our project before beginning to wet felt. Here is a guide to how we prepare the different fibre formats prior to felting. It's worth noting that, whichever format you are using, you'll find it easier to pull a wisp or piece of fibre straight from the top of a strip or length with a loose grip (and dry hands). This gives you a piece with wispy edges, which is better for fibre integration in felting. The standard practice for laying out fibre is to overlap wispy pieces, to create even layers which build up into an integrated shape.

Range of dyed and undyed carded wool batt fibre.

Undyed and dyed carded wool sliver fibre.

Plain commercially dyed and variegated hand-dyed Merino combed wool tops fibre.

Step by Step
Preparing Carded Batt Fibre

Step 1: Separating the batt into thin layers.

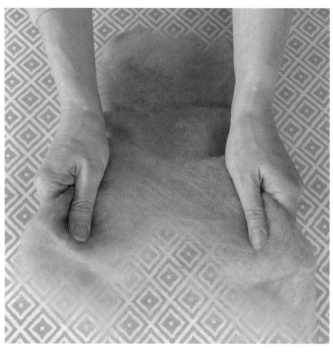

Step 2: Tearing a layer into strips.

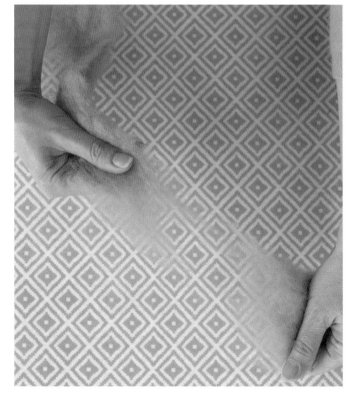

Step 3: Pulling smaller pieces from a strip.

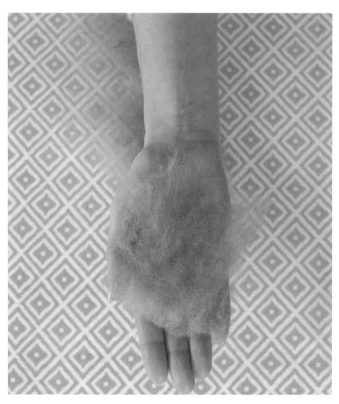

Step 4: A prepared, palm-sized piece.

Preparing Carded Sliver Fibre

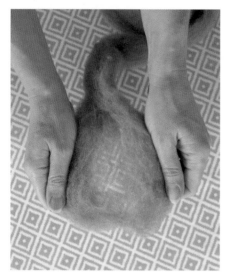

Step 1: Dividing the sliver length in half (if necessary).

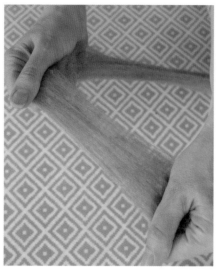

Step 2: Pulling smaller pieces from the sliver length.

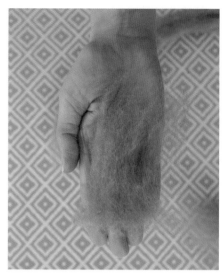

Step 3: A prepared palm-sized piece.

Preparing Combed Tops Fibre

Step 1: Pulling a wisp of fibre from the length of tops.

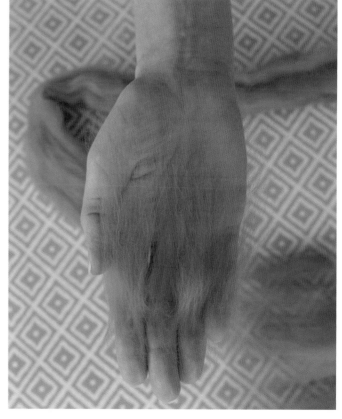

Step 2: A prepared wisp of tops fibre.

Wool fibre for felting on a ball

Any of the wool fibre forms will felt (as long as they have not been specifically treated to not felt, such as superwash wool tops), but for felting on a ball it is carded wool fibre which we are primarily going to use, in batt and sliver form, using a papier mâché layout technique (*see* Chapter 2). The basic reason for this is that carded wool fibre, when wet and torn into pieces, maintains a manageable structure which works well for the wet layout technique we're using, to achieve a tight, even, overlapping layout. In contrast, a wisp of combed tops fibre is very delicate and has little structure to it, which makes wetting and adding it to the ball, and building up the thickness of layers we need, much more difficult. So it is not so much the fibre breed as the format of the fibre which makes the difference to successful felting on a ball.

However, although you can felt anything you like out of any fibre, it is always worth considering the end purpose of your felt and which fibre breed would be most suitable for it. A coarser fibre like Bergschaf, which felts well together in a thick layer and will hold its shape and structure, is ideally suited to creating a hardwearing bag or basket. Whereas finer and softer Merino, which doesn't felt as well in a thicker layer, is more suited to creating a fine, drapey scarf. The nature of most felting on a ball projects is to create 3D felt which has good structure and thickness, requiring a coarser fibre. So the upshot is that carded wool fibre, of a coarser thickness, is the most structurally suited fibre to use for this technique.

It is, of course, possible to use Merino combed wool tops for felting on a ball, so I have included a project in Chapter 5 to make a Nuno Silk Cowl, a more delicate item with drape which makes best use of Merino's soft and fine qualities and only requires a single thin layer of fibre. You can also use tops fibres as a decorative layer or area on the ball as part of your embellishments, or you could card the tops fibres yourself or create prefelts from them to use in the layout, which would give them better structure and make them more manageable when wet. Merino is also available commercially in carded wool batt fibre form or as prefelt.

There are other ways we can use combed wool tops fibre too, which seems to be down to the difference between large commercial and smaller-scale fibre producers. With hand-dyed, combed wool tops, I've found that the fibres tend to felt together slightly during the dyeing process, giving them a less wispy structure and hence making them easier to use with the wet layout method of felting on a ball. Directionally, the fibres still have a uniformity which makes it harder to achieve a very even layout, but you can compensate for this by laying the wisps on the ball in different directions. You'll see that I've used a Corriedale version in the Sari Silk Bowl Project in Chapter 5. So keep an eye out for different wool fibres, especially at craft markets where you will find more independent small-scale suppliers, as you might find that the way materials have been treated might make them more suitable to use for felting on a ball.

Embellishment Materials

There are lots of surface design materials available that we can use to decorate our felt, but I'm focusing here on the ones I've used in the projects and which work well with the felting on a ball process.

Wool yarns

Adding wool yarns is a simple way of incorporating highlights of colour, pattern and texture into wet felting. Because they have the same feltable properties as wool fibre (yarn is spun from wool fibre), wool yarns and fibre will bond happily together, with the yarns being drawn into the fibre and becoming embedded. Aim for yarns with a high wool content, and the hairier the better as this helps the bonding. Mohair yarns are excellent for this reason, and can be found in lots of different textural varieties, such as straight, loop or bouclé, slubby and mixed with sparkly fibres. I also like to use chunky wool yarns, which are either straight thick or thick and thin in structure, which give great coverage on the ball and are reliable felters. Art yarns are chunky yarns available from artisan suppliers which often have interesting twists, slubs and other elements incorporated in them and provide amazing texture.

Mohair wool yarns in straight, loop/bouclé and slub versions.

Mohair wool yarn blends with metallic fibres.

Chunky thick and thin wool yarns.

Curly wool locks

Some sheep breeds have distinctive long locks with a well-defined crimp or curl which is preserved during processing. They are available dyed and undyed and can be used to create great texture and pattern in wet felting, either kept in their defined curls or wisped out for broader coverage.

Silk fibres

Silk fibres come in a variety of formats (including tops, hankies, caps and bricks), both dyed and undyed, and are perfect for adding colour and a subtle sheen to wet felting projects. Simply peel them apart (in the case of hankies or caps) and spread them out, or cut pieces from them before wisping, lay them on the ball and spray to secure. Although they don't have feltable properties, their fineness makes it easy for the wool fibre to bond with them. Silk fibres are a type of protein fibre, along with wool, which originates from an animal.

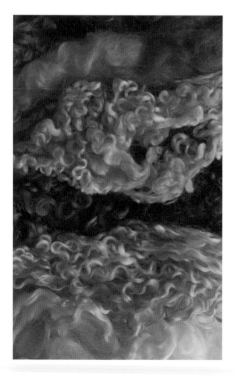

Hand-dyed Teeswater and Wensleydale long curly wool locks.

Hand-dyed silk hankies (square layers), caps (bowl-shaped layers) and bricks (thicker pieces of combed silk tops).

Plant fibres

There are lots of plant-derived fibres, such as bamboo and viscose (made from cellulose/wood pulp), which are similar to silk fibres and work in the same way by adding sheen to the surface of the felt. Like silk fibres, they felt easily with wool fibre.

Plain and variegated dyed bamboo tops (left) and plain dyed viscose tops (right).

Wool fibre blends

There is a vast array of wool fibre blends available, in all sorts of combinations, from both large-scale commercial suppliers, where you'll find repeatable blends such as Merino combed tops mixed with a lustre fibre like silk, and more artisan suppliers, where you'll find hand-carded blends and one-off art batts (a rolled-up batt) and rolags (a fine carded layer rolled up and shaped into a spiral). A fine, wispy layer of blended fibres is simple to spread out and add to the ball and will bond easily with the main wool fibre, as well as adding interesting colour, texture and pattern to it.

Hand-carded wool fibre blends in batt form, including sari silk blends, art batts and a rolag, and commercial blends in tops form.

Tweed-effect tops blends comprising South American wool and viscose fibres.

Prefelt

Prefelt (or pre-felt) is the term for felt which is partially felted, where the wool fibres have only just bonded together and not gone through the full felting process. It is available commercially in sheets, or as ribbon, and can be used as an alternative to laying out fibre for a project, or to cut out and incorporate pieces from as part of a surface design. You can make your own or use offcuts from other felting projects where you might have stopped at prefelt stage. You can also use finished felt offcuts in a similar way beneath the surface of a fibre layout to help create raised areas.

Rolls of extra fine Merino prefelt ribbon in different widths.

Handmade felt (top) and prefelt (bottom) offcuts which can be incorporated into wet felting projects.

Silk fabric

Silk and other open-weave fabrics can be combined with wool fibre to create nuno felt, which is felt with a bonded surface layer of fabric. *See* Chapter 5 for further details.

Finishing Materials

As well as some specific items needed to complete some of the projects, such as a cushion pad for the Mandala Crochet Cushion Project in Chapter 3, here are some of the other materials needed to finish the wet felted projects in this book.

Hand-dyed Margilan silk fabrics.

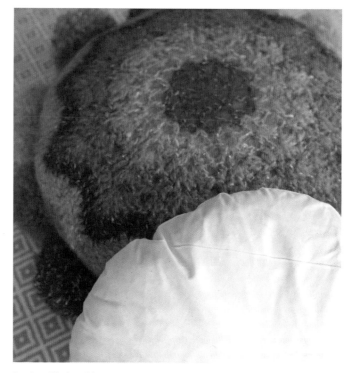

Feather-filled pad for completing a cushion project.

Closure materials

Some felting projects will need a closure of some kind to complete the project, which can also help to give a professional-looking finish. Using simple hand-sewing techniques we can add zips and clasps to items like cushions and bags – *see* Chapter 7 for further details.

Bag hardware

Metal rings are used in bagmaking for attaching elements like handles, straps and closures. In wet felting projects we can use fibre to felt the rings securely in place so that, when the bag or backpack is finished, we can simply attach straps to or through the rings to complete the project.

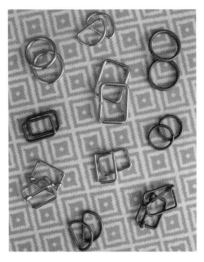

Metal bag rings in a variety of shapes, sizes and finishes.

Selection of closure materials: zips, magnetic clasp fasteners and turn-lock/tuck lock clasps.

Embroidery and machine sewing threads for hand-sewing closure materials.

Examples of bag straps with lobster clasp ends for easy attaching to a ring.

CHAPTER 2

GETTING STARTED

The basic technique of wet felting to create felt is quite straightforward: take wool fibre, add soapy water, agitate the fibres to bond them together and you'll eventually end up with felt. It's worth appreciating that wet felting is a natural process, and we're not forcing the fibres to create felt and having to struggle to do it, so in that sense it's not difficult or complicated to achieve. But if we want to create a more refined result, then that's where understanding more about the process, and being able to deploy targeted techniques at different stages of that process, will help us to manipulate and elevate our felt to the beautiful pieces we want to create. So this chapter delves further into the technique of wet felting, and specifically wet felting on a ball, to introduce you to the process and quickly get you started. It also includes lots of tips for successfully navigating each stage, which I've developed through my own exploration of felting on a ball.

THE WET FELTING PROCESS

Wet felting is the process of bonding wool fibres using water. It is made possible by the structure of wool fibre, which has microscopic scales along each individual fibre strand. By wetting and then agitating the fibre, using techniques like rubbing, the scales start to open up and lock together. The more we continue to agitate the fibre, the tighter the fibres lock together, until eventually they turn into a dense mass of fibres which cannot be pulled apart, which is felt. The addition of soap, which helps to open up the fibre scales and smooth the process of agitation, and heat (usually provided by warm water), which helps to speed up the felting, are standard aspects which will help the process along.

There are three main stages to creating felt, which each involve different actions:

- **The layout stage:** This is when you lay out your dry wool fibre on your work surface, along with any embellishment materials you are using, to create your design. Once ready, you would then wet the fibre with soapy water and move on to the next stage.
- **The felting stage:** This is when you start to gently agitate the wet fibre, causing it to just begin bonding to create an initial, loose version of felt called prefelt. The fibres will be developing a collective 'skin' and appear more as an integrated whole. However, they are very delicate at this stage and could still be pulled apart, and haven't yet started to compact and shrink (hence there is no strength yet to the fibre piece).
- **The fulling stage:** This is when you increase the level of agitation to encourage the fibres to bond completely and, as they lock together more tightly, the loose prefelt shrinks to create a firm, strong felt. The felt will feel thicker with a more textured, wrinkled, bumpy surface. You'd then rinse out the soap and water, reshape your felt and leave it to dry.

It's worth noting that there isn't a clear transition point when prefelt becomes felt, and prefelt itself can be a broad category from very loose fibres which are barely holding together to fibres which appear well combined into a more solid piece, although overall it is still quite delicate. As a very general principle, however, I would consider the prefelt stage to be any point up until the piece starts to shrink.

You might also wonder when your felt is finished. Again, there is no fixed point to mark this, it is more a collection of signs, such as shrinkage, thickness, feeling very firm and having a textured surface like crocodile skin. It is also down to personal preference and the end use: a piece of decorative felt which will be put in a picture frame and never handled doesn't need to be felted as much as a bag, which will get lots of wear. You might also deliberately want to stop felting earlier if you find that your embellishments are sinking too far into the finished felt and being 'eaten' by it and you still want to be able to see them. As a general rule, however, and because most of the felt I make is very structural, I would consider a piece to be fully felted once it has lost any squidginess, feels very firm and is holding its structure well.

As well as choosing your wool fibre and any embellishment materials, a key consideration before you start any project is shrinkage. As the fibres lock together, they compact (to literally take up less space), which means that the finished felt will always be smaller than the fibre layout you start with, on average by around 25 per cent. You might think of it as an unhelpful complication, but bear in mind that the shrinkage is what gives our finished felt its thickness, structure, hardiness and texture.

WET FELTING ON A BALL

Felting on a ball follows the same overall process and stages as any wet felting project, but we're working in 3D on a ball so we need to adapt some of our techniques. We're going to run through the whole felting on a ball process step by step shortly in this chapter, but before we do I'd like to highlight the key techniques which we'll be using, some of which are specific to felting on a ball and hence different to other felting techniques you might have encountered previously. These techniques follow the three main stages of the process outlined above.

The Layout Stage
Layout order
A key aspect to bear in mind at the start of any felting on a ball project is that, for the majority of projects, we are laying out our surface design and wool fibre inside out. So we will add the embellishment materials to the ball first, followed by several layers of wool fibre, ending up with the inside layer of the project on the outside. The reason for this is in order to protect the design. If we worked logically, starting with the inside layer and finishing with the embellishments, there's a risk when we move on to agitating the ball that we will disrupt our carefully prepared design. By working inside out we can protect it, as well as help the embellishments to bond with the fibre by keeping them very tightly sandwiched in place between the ball and the fibre.

Shrinkage
Exact shrinkage is not so important for felting on a ball when we are creating items which don't have a critical end size, such as bowls, bags and baskets. However, of course there are projects, notably hats, for which it is crucial to get the size right, particularly the starting size. Often in wet felting we might create a small, 2D sample piece to establish the shrinkage rate of the fibre, which we can then apply to our chosen project to help calculate the correct starting size, but there are many other variables that will also affect the finished size, such as: how much fibre you use, the type and amount of embellishments you include, how much you full the felt and in which directions, and how you shape it. So although you can have a good stab at calculating the likely shrinkage using a small test piece, ultimately I've found that the best approach is to do a full test on the ball with all those variables, making a sample version and then tweaking the sizes and other variables to achieve your desired outcome. You can use the starting sizes of the projects in this book as a guide to make your test sample.

To calculate the exact shrinkage from a test piece made on the ball, the easiest method is to use the starting and finishing circumference sizes of the test version. Using our bowl sample later in this chapter as an example (and I'm using just metric figures here for simplicity):

- The starting ball size is 76cm.
- The finished bowl size is 58cm.
- The difference in size is 18cm (76 − 58 = 18).
- Difference in size of 18cm divided by starting size of 76cm multiplied by 100 (18 ÷ 76 × 100) = shrinkage rate of approximately 24 per cent.

This isn't an exact calculation because it doesn't account for the different heights and depths that we could have shaped our bowl to, which would change the circumference size, but it gives a good approximate figure.

Once you have the shrinkage rate, you can then work out the reverse percentage, which will tell us what 100 per cent (in other words, the starting size) of our target size would be before the shrinkage. So, using the same example, if we decided that we would like our finished bowl to be 66cm in circumference instead:

- Shrinkage rate is 24 per cent.
- Remaining percentage size is 76 per cent (100 − 24 = 76).
- Target bowl size is 66cm.
- Target bowl size of 66cm divided by remaining percentage size of 76 multiplied by 100 (66 ÷ 76 × 100) = starting size of 87cm.

These simple calculations will give you an approximate starting size to work with for your final version. Just bear in mind that the many variables will have a huge impact on the shrinkage, so if size is important then making samples using the same wool fibre, materials and shaping as your desired outcome is your most accurate way of getting nearer to the results you want.

Papier mâché layout technique

Although we would normally lay out dry fibre for a project, setting the overall shape and thickness before adding water, as we're working in 3D we have to work slightly differently. You can imagine that if we put dry fibre on top of a smooth ball it will simply fall off. Also, if we used a sheet of carded wool batt fibre and tried to place it around the ball, you can see that it wouldn't fit well as there would be excess fibre at the top and bottom where the ball narrows. So we're going to use a completely different process for laying out fibre, which involves putting small wet fibre pieces onto the ball instead: the small pieces enable us to get a tight fit around the spherical shape, and the wetness will enable them to temporarily stick on the ball. I call this technique the papier mâché layout, as it's very similar to the process of building up a papier mâché shape using small pieces of overlapping paper soaked in glue.

Step by Step

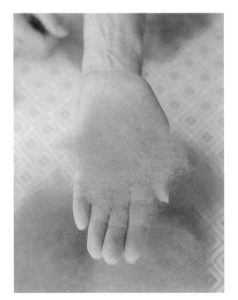

Step 1: Tear the carded wool fibre into palm-sized pieces of equal thickness.

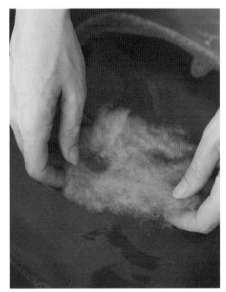

Step 2: Dunk a piece of fibre into lukewarm soapy water to soak it.

Step 3: Gently lift the fibre out of the water with your fingers, keeping the edges wispy.

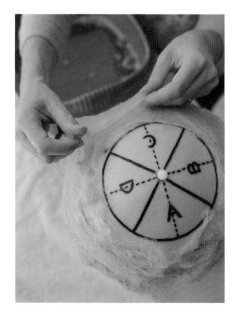

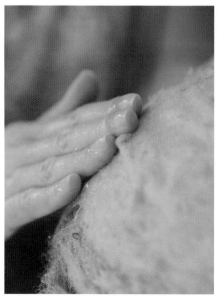

Step 4: Place the fibre onto the ball, on top of any embellishment materials.

Step 5: Smooth out the wispy fibre edges and any lumps.

Step 6: Repeat with further fibre pieces, overlapping slightly, until the ball is evenly covered.

The Felting Stage

Push rub technique

Once our wet fibre layout is complete, we can move on to the first stage of agitating the fibre to encourage all the individual pieces to start bonding together. As the fibre is still so delicate at this point, we first need to cover the fibre to protect it (using thin plastic and two layers of tights) and our agitation needs to start gently. Rubbing the fibre is a standard wet felting technique we might deploy at this stage. However, rubbing the ball evenly all over with our hands for many minutes would take quite some physical effort. To make rubbing the whole ball easier, if we push it around within a snugly fitting bowl we have the benefit of it being rubbed by our hands as well as the sides of the bowl where it makes contact. That way, we get maximum rubbing for minimum effort. I call this the push rub technique: each push rub equates to one push of the ball within the bowl (we push and the bowl rubs).

My standard recipe for most projects is three rounds of 400 push rubs, unwrapping the fibre in between rounds to make adjustments such as folding over the top fibre edge, to create a neat, rounded edge, and to check the fibre overall for neatness and wetness. It may sound like a lot of push rubs, but each round of 400 takes on average four minutes to complete. Start slowly, to avoid pushing the fibre so hard initially that it moves position on the ball, and build up to pushing it more firmly by the third round once the fibre is feeling firmer.

The push rub technique: moving the ball within the bowl to rub the fibre all over.

After three rounds of 400 push rubs, making 1,200 in total, the fibre should be feeling more integrated and firm and be developing a smooth skin. If there is any fluffiness or pieces of fibre still lifting from the surface (check this throughout the rounds), it is worth adding more soapy water (the consistency should be soapy and sodden throughout) and completing a further round. It doesn't help to move the process on to a higher level of agitation before the fibre is ready.

Bouncing technique

After rubbing the fibre, it should be feeling more bonded and therefore ready to respond to increased agitation through bouncing. Bouncing is a very specific technique afforded to us through our use of a ball. When each bounce hits the work surface, it sends an agitating shock throughout the fibre around the ball. Fortunately we don't have to actually try and bounce the fibre-covered ball as you would a basketball, an easier method is to hold the tights tightly above the ball and bounce the ball on a hard work surface, without moving the ball around too much (to conserve your energy). You can very quickly, in around two minutes, complete the 500 bounces in each round of four that I recommend at this stage.

Although bouncing has an effect on all the fibre around the ball, it has a bigger impact on the area of fibre which is hitting the work surface. To even out this impact, I like to vary the placement of the ball in the tights each round, alternating from plug up, to plug down, and from side A (or B) down to side C (or D) down.

Generally I would complete four rounds of bouncing, especially when dealing with a large amount of fibre which will take longer to fully bond, or when using a slow-felting wool fibre

The bouncing technique: bouncing the ball on a hard work surface.

breed. However, sometimes three or even two rounds are enough, depending on how well the fibre is felting. If at any point the fibre feels tight around the ball, the surface feels coarser and the top edge is visibly receding, these are good indications that it is felting well. One thing you could do before the next round is let a little air out of the ball (just enough to get a finger inside) so that the felt can start shrinking without being constrained by the ball. If you have a lot of tricky embellishment materials, it might also be worth stopping the bouncing slightly earlier and remove the ball so that you can get your hands directly onto the embellishments to rub them and encourage them to bond with the fibre before it becomes too felted.

The Fulling Stage

Once we remove the ball, our fibre has turned into a well-progressed prefelt and will feel more substantial and integrated. It's a good idea at this point to give it a warm soaking and rub the embellishments on the inside to ensure they are fully bonded. Then you can start deploying fulling techniques, at an even greater level of agitation, the aims of which are to shrink the felt whilst shaping it into its final form. As we are no longer working on the ball, these are largely the same as for any other sort of wet felting, although because we have made a 3D hollow form there is a greater emphasis on techniques which will maintain a 3D shape.

Throwing is the main shrinking technique. To maintain a rounded shape like a basket, I recommend throwing by spinning the felt around on its side and hitting the work surface to mark each throw, either by keeping a hand inside the felt, supported by the other hand outside, or using both hands to move it around. Letting go as you throw the whole felt down flat on the table is something you might do to create a flatter shape, such as with a cushion. Once the felt has started to shrink, you can alternate throwing with more shaping techniques such as stretching the inside and rubbing the sides for a more rounded shape, and rolling it on itself for a flatter shape and to shrink the felt in a specific direction. If your felt is shrinking slowly, you might also deploy actions like scrunching the felt and giving it hot and cold rinses under the tap. It is a combination of these fulling techniques which shrinks and moves the felt into its final form. Then, once you are happy, rinse the felt until the water is clear of soap, wrap it in a towel to dry it off, reshape it and leave it to air dry. I also try to leave a small window of shrinking until the rinsing stage, as the rinsing and drying actions are all still agitating the fibre.

Step by Step

Step 1: Throwing with one hand inside: to shrink whilst keeping a more rounded shape.

Step 2: Throwing with both hands outside: to shrink whilst keeping a more rounded shape.

Step 3: Throwing and letting go: to shrink whilst creating a more flattened shape.

Step 4: Stretching: to widen the shape and smooth the surface.

Step 5: Rubbing: to create shape and smooth the surface.

Step 6: Rolling: to shrink the felt in the direction of rolling.

Timescales to Complete a Project

It's worth clarifying that you don't need to complete all of the stages above in one go, you can break up the process to make it physically easier and to accommodate what time you have available. The only stage which really needs to be completed in one session is the layout, because any embellishments need to be covered by the fibre, and then the fibre ideally needs to be covered by the plastic and the tights, to keep everything protected and held in place. But you could aim to prepare all your materials and fibre the day before, and start the actual felting the day after completing the layout (although ideally I like to complete a couple of rounds of push rubs before leaving it, just to start everything holding together). Once you remove the ball you could give any embellishments a rub and then leave the fulling until yet another day. At whatever stage you begin again, just rewet the fibre with fresh soapy water before continuing.

Use of Soapy Water

A final point about the felting on a ball process, which I can't emphasise enough, is about using plenty of soapy water. As fast as we are adding water to the fibre, it is dripping, drying or being bounced out. A warm environment, certain dye colours and using natural, undyed wool are further variables which might make the fibre dry out more quickly. Water (assisted by soap) is the key element which makes a successful wet felted felt. So throughout the process, you should be constantly checking that the fibre is in a soapy, sodden state and, if not, adding more soapy water, either spraying it on during layout or pouring it on/dunking it after prefelt stage. If your fibre is peeling off the ball during layout or your prefelt/felt at any point feels dry, doesn't appear to be bonding well or isn't shrinking, then the addition of soapy water is usually the answer.

The fibre should be soapy and sodden throughout the wet felting process.

EMBELLISHED BOWL SAMPLE PROJECT

Before we get into some final tips for felting on a ball, let's start off with an overview of the main stages of the basic process to give you a feel for exactly what's involved and get you started quickly if you're keen to dive right in. We're going to run through all the steps of making a simple bowl from scratch, from marking up guidelines on the ball to laying out embellishments and wool fibre, before felting your bowl to completion. A bowl is the most straightforward project for felting on a ball, as it doesn't have any extra felted parts (like handles and flaps) and is easy to shape as you are largely keeping the same shape as the ball. I've also included two types of embellishment materials, wool yarns and blended fibres, to show you how to incorporate different types of embellishment in felting on a ball projects.

Hopefully this overview will ignite your interest in the process as well as prepare you for more detail as we delve further into each stage in the rest of this chapter. I also hope it will act as a good basic reference guide and reminder of the process whenever you're approaching a new project or if you need a refresher. (NB: If your ball won't reach 76cm/30in) in circumference, use one of the fibre recipes for the layer amounts from one of the other projects using a similar ball size.)

The finished bowl weighs approximately 115g and measures approximately 17cm wide × 21cm high (6.75in × 8.25in), and 58cm (23in) in circumference.

WHAT YOU WILL NEED

Materials

- Approximately 90g of carded wool fibre in your chosen colours: 30g per main layer (×3)
- I used Finnwool carded wool batt fibre in the following combination:

Layout Element	Colour	Amount
Layer 1	Yellow	10g
	Orange	10g
	Turquoise	10g
Layer 2	Yellow	10g
	Orange	10g
	Turquoise	10g
Layer 3	Turquoise	30g

- Approximately 3–5m (10–16ft) each of at least five wool yarns (I used a variety of mohair, mohair boucle and slubby mohair yarns in yellow, orange, pink and turquoise shades)
- Approximately 5–10g of hand-carded, blended fibres (I used a mix of Bluefaced Leicester and alpaca fibre with recycled sari silk, in yellow and blue shades)

Equipment

- Green felting ball, inflated to 76cm (30in) circumference
- Inflating pump
- Small round bowl to prop up the ball
- Large bowl of any size to hold the washing-up liquid and warm water solution
- 28cm (11in) minimum internal diameter round or square bowl (to push rub the ball within)
- Two pairs of medium/large (102–122cm/40–48in hips) tights/pantyhose, 20 denier (see Chapter 1 for preparation)
- 100cm × 55cm (40in × 22in) piece of thin plastic
- Washing-up/dishwashing liquid
- Olive oil soap
- Spray bottle (containing washing-up liquid and warm water solution)
- Ball brause
- Several large towels
- Several small/tea towels
- Scales
- Tape measure
- Permanent marker pen
- Small scissors

Step by Step
Preparing the felting ball

Step 2: Marking up the felting ball

With a permanent marker pen and tape measure, mark up the top circle and middle design lines, top placement lines and base centre point.

Step 1: Inflating the felting ball

Using a pump, inflate the ball to 76cm (30in) in circumference. Refer to the measurements in Chapter 1 for marking up the green ball at this size.

Preparing the materials

Step 3: Assembling your colour palette

Gather together your carded wool fibre, wool yarns and embellishment fibres to create a pleasing colour palette of at least two or three main colours.

Step 4: Weighing the fibre

Weigh 30g of carded wool fibre for each of the three layers (90g in total). I've divided layers one and two into three colours, with one colour for layer three.

Step 5: Preparing the fibre

Tear all fibre into palm-sized pieces. For fibre in batt form, first peel the layers into thinner sheets, tear the sheets into strips and then into small pieces. Put aside.

Preparing the equipment

Step 6: Preparing the work surface

Lay out a large towel as your working area and have more available to replace the first one once soaked and for drying the finished felt after rinsing.

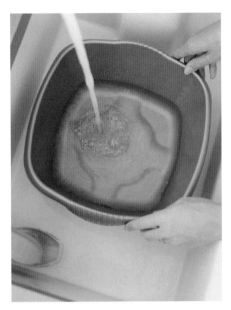

Step 7: Preparing the bowls

Use a small bowl to prop up the ball. Half fill a large bowl with lukewarm water for soaking the yarns. Have a 32cm (12.5in) diameter bowl ready for the rubbing stage.

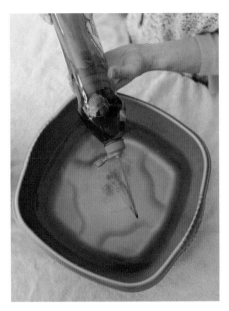

Step 8: Preparing the soapy solution

Put a long squirt of washing-up liquid into the large bowl of water, gently stir and ensure the water feels slimy.

Step 9: Preparing the tights

To prepare the tights, turn them inside out and tie a knot in each leg approximately 7.5cm (3in) down from the gusset centre join. Cut off the leg excess.

Step 10: Assembling the other equipment

Gather together the rest of the initial equipment, such as the spray bottle containing lukewarm water and a long squirt of washing-up liquid, thin plastic and scissors.

Laying out the embellishment materials

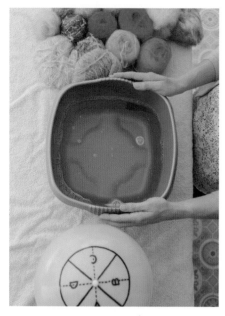

Step 11: Preparing the working area

Working on the towel, place the bowl of soapy water directly in front of you, with the yarns on one side and the ball on the other in its propping-up bowl.

Step 12: Soaking the first yarn

Take the first yarn, unwind at least 1m (40in) and dunk it in the soapy water, without cutting it and keeping hold of the loose end.

Step 13: Adding the first yarn to the ball

Starting with the loose end, wrap the soapy yarn around the ball in a wavy organic line at least three times. Unwind and soak more yarn as needed, then cut off.

Step 14: Adding more yarns

Repeat to add further yarns, varying the placement each time to avoid too much overlapping in the same place, until you have built up a pleasing design.

Step 15: Adding embellishment fibres

Spread/wisp out the embellishment fibres into long strips or smaller pieces and place them dry on top of the yarns, ensuring an even thickness.

Step 16: Securing the embellishment fibres

Press the fibres into the wet ball to hold them in place as you add them, then spray with soapy water to secure.

Laying out the wool fibre

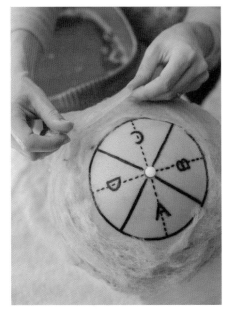

Step 17: Adding the first wool fibre piece

From the 30g fibre allocation for layer one, take a piece of fibre, soak it in soapy water, ensure it is spread out and place it directly on top of the embellishments.

Step 18: Adding the first wool fibre layer

Repeat with the rest of the allocation. Overlap fibre pieces, smooth out any lumps and cover the entire ball in as even a layer as possible up to the top circle line.

Step 19: Adding the rest of the wool fibre

Repeat to add the layer two and three fibre allocations. Pat regularly to check evenness and add additional fibre pieces as necessary to thicken thin areas.

Rubbing the fibre

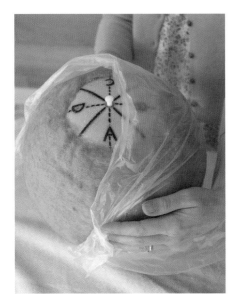

Step 20: Covering the fibre in plastic

Generously spray the fibre all over and wrap in thin plastic, without completely covering the ball so that water can still get inside the plastic.

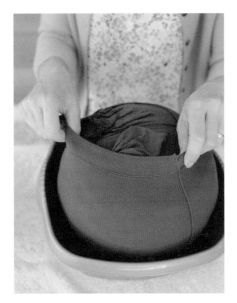

Step 21: Placing the ball in tights

Stretch one pair of tights over the rubbing bowl and place the ball inside, then repeat with the second pair, covering the area of the ball not covered by the first pair.

Step 22: Rubbing the fibre

With the ball inside the bowl, pour on soapy water to soak the tights. Gently push the ball around within the bowl, making contact with the sides, for 400 pushes/push rubs.

Step 23: Neatening the top edge

Peel the tights back over the edges of the bowl and peel back the plastic. Fluff up the open top edge of the fibre and fold it outwards. Spray and rub to secure.

Step 24: Completing the rubbing

Replace the plastic and tights and repeat the round of 400 push rubs twice more, pushing more firmly and checking/rubbing the top edge after each round.

Step 25: Bouncing the ball

With the ball still in tights and plastic, bounce it 500 times on the work surface. Remove the tights/plastic to check the top edge. Add more soapy water if dry.

Fulling the fibre

Step 26: Completing the bouncing

Replace the tights/plastic and complete a further 500 bounces three more times. If the fibre feels very tight around the ball, deflate it slightly before the final round.

Step 27: Removing the ball

Remove the tights and plastic, deflate the ball and remove it from the prefelt bowl shape. Give the inside of the bowl a good soapy shower and soap your hands.

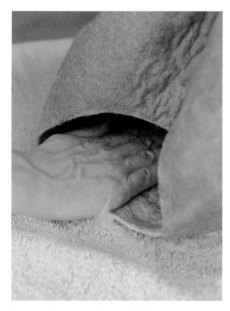

Step 28: Securing the embellishments

Rub your fingers over the embellishments to check they are adhering to the inside of the bowl. If still loose, rub them with wet, soapy hands until they feel more secure.

Step 29: Soaking the fibre

Replace the original bowl of soapy water with fresh, warm/hand hot soapy water. Completely soak the prefelt bowl and place it on the towel on your work surface.

Step 30: Throwing the felt

Put your hand inside the bowl and spin it around on its sides so that it hits the work surface 100 times but maintains the round shape. Rub the inside embellishments.

Step 31: Continuing to throw the felt

Reshape the bowl and flatten the base, then repeat a further two rounds of 100 throws, rubbing the embellishments and reshaping the bowl after each round.

Step 32: Shaping the felt

Turn the bowl right side out and throw a further two or three rounds of 100 until the bowl feels thicker and is holding its shape. Stretch inside and rub the sides to shape.

Finishing the felt

Step 33: Rinsing the felt

Rinse the felt in warm water until clear of soap. Gently squeeze to remove excess water, then roll up in a dry towel and reshape.

Step 34: Final shaping

To create a rounded shape and stretch the surface smooth, reinsert the felting ball and inflate it as far as possible. Rub the sides smooth, deflate the ball and air dry.

FURTHER TIPS FOR FELTING ON A BALL

Now that you understand the basic felting on a ball process to create an embellished bowl, here are some specific tips I've developed in my own practice, usually in an attempt to make a certain aspect easier or work better, so I'm sharing these below to help you achieve success with the projects. They are organised under the same headings as the sample bowl. I hope they will answer any remaining questions as to why I recommend doing things in a certain way, as well as head off any potential issues you might encounter before they arise. As with any kind of felting, it's worth pointing out that there's no single way of felting on a ball, but I'm sharing the methods I've developed over many years which have worked for me. So if you're new to the process, then you might like to follow these quite closely initially. But if you're already experienced with felting or felting on a ball, then you might want to adapt some of my methods to suit you and the materials you enjoy using, and you might also pick up some new tips to help finesse your own techniques.

Preparing the felting ball

Never pick up the ball by the plug! Or if you do, always support it at the bottom with your other hand, especially when it is weighed down by fibre.

The top plug will protrude. Most of the balls I use have top plugs which protrude slightly, but this doesn't seem to adversely affect the rubbing or bouncing stages so don't worry too much about it. Don't feel that you have to force the plug all the way in as they aren't necessarily designed for that and it might cause you great difficulty removing it. If you're concerned about the plug sticking out or sticking into an area of your fibre layout, just cover it with a small piece of bubble wrap and remember that any indentations during felting are not permanent.

Preparing the materials

Choosing the wool fibre

This will depend on the outcome you want, whether you're looking for a hardwearing fibre to give a thick, structural result for a bag (for which a coarser carded wool fibre like Bergschaf would work well) or a fine, soft fibre for a scarf (for which Merino tops would be perfect). It might also just come down to what fibre you have a lot of, and which colour you might have available. It's worth experimenting with different fibres, as you will find that some will give a tighter and stiffer result (such as Finnwool), whereas others might be spongier and more flexible

(such as Maori-Bergschaf), and hence they might each be more suited to different projects.

Choosing the right embellishment materials

To increase your chances of success in bonding your embellishment materials to the wool fibre, and for a more enjoyable felting experience, use the most reliable materials that you can. So a hairy mohair or loose spun 100 per cent wool yarn, or Margilan silk fabric, are likely to give you a better (that is, easier and more successful) result than a tightly-spun, smooth, wool/acrylic mix yarn or polyester organza fabric. It doesn't mean you can't use other materials or things you're not sure of, but it's always worth testing them first or being prepared to do some extra bonding work when you remove the ball.

Choosing colours

As a general guideline, I find that including three main colours in any project gives a good balance of interest. A simple way of approaching a project is to use one or two main colours for your fibre background (or you might use similar shades of just one colour), with at least two main colours in your embellishments, which act as highlights on top of your wool fibre. Because of the way the wool fibre bonds with the embellishment materials, covering them with a fine haze of fibre in order to lock them in place, this brings a uniformity/harmony to the design to bring it all together. The only thing to note is that, as a result, the embellishment colours will be toned down by this halo of wool fibre on top. So I recommend increasing the vibrancy of the embellishment colours to compensate for this.

Weighing fibre

If you want to be able to repeat a project successfully, then getting into the habit of weighing your fibre and the individual fibre components (such as the weight of each layer) will enable you to produce consistent results, as well as help you work out where to tweak things in your next version if you decide there's an aspect you'd like to improve.

Organising your fibre

Some of the larger projects use a lot of wool fibre for different components, which is very easy to muddle up once you get started on your layout. So I weigh and prepare all my fibre first, divided up into different bowls or bags. As you ideally want to complete all your layout for a project in one session, having your fibre ready to go is a big asset. It also helps not having to chop and change between working wet and working dry, as trying to prepare fibre with wet hands is difficult. Another advantage is that your fibre preparation can be done in advance so that you're not having to complete every stage of a big project in one day.

Preparing the equipment

Waterproofing your working area

Be aware that water dripping is an occupational hazard with this technique so a waterproof surface under the towel is essential. An alternative to working on a towel is using a boot tray or similar which will catch the water.

Arranging your working area

To avoid dripping water over your materials during layout (which, particularly with a pile of wool fibre, makes it a bit unmanageable), keep your water bowl in the middle with your materials kept dry one side and the ball the other.

Water temperature

This differs at different stages of the process. I generally start with warmish or lukewarm water in my bowl and spray bottle, to avoid any risk of a high water temperature prematurely felting the fibre. It's cooled by the time I start using it, and by the time we're removing the ball it's pretty cold. I don't warm it up throughout the felting stage; if I need to top up the water I add more cool water, so the temperature is consistent. Once we move to the fulling stage, however, and we've removed the ball, that is the time to warm up the prefelt with fresh warm soapy water because we want to use the heat to help with rubbing the embellishments and starting the fulling. Later, once shrinkage has started and you're happy that both fibre and embellishments are adhering well, you might assist that process with alternate hot and cold rinses if you think your project needs a shrinking/thickening boost.

Laying Out the Embellishment Materials

Remember that you're working inside out

If you are using different embellishment materials, just be aware that whatever you place on the ball first will be the outermost and most visible embellishment. So if there is an order to your design you might want to make a note of this in advance.

Dunking versus spraying

All the materials and fibre laid on the ball need to be wet and soapy to keep them in place. As a general rule, if an embellishment material has good structure to it, such as wool yarn or a piece of sari silk, then you can use the dunk and place method to lay it on the ball. But if it is a fine or wispy material, such as tops fibres, curly wool locks or Margilan silk fabric, which loses its structural integrity when wet and becomes unmanageable, then placing the item on the ball and spraying to secure is a better option.

Keeping your placement wavy

Embellishment materials bond most successfully when they are loose, wispy, spread out and laid in an organic, wavy pattern. The looseness enables the wool fibre to bond with the embellishments more easily. Yarns in particular, if laid in a continuous circle around the ball, can become taut, which makes it very hard for the wool fibres to bond with them. So keep your yarn designs organic if possible, or use shorter lengths, and wisp out your other materials as much as you can.

Keeping embellishments away from the top edge

Whichever line you are using as your top edge marks the top edge of the fibre. Keep your thicker embellishments, such as yarn and fabric, at least 2.5cm (1in) lower than this. (NB: This doesn't apply to fine fibres, which you can broadly treat the same as the wool fibre.) There are two reasons for this. Firstly, we will be folding the top edge outwards to thicken and neaten it, so we don't want embellishments interfering with the fold. Secondly, because the fibre opening has no way of being held in place by the ball, you'll find that the top edge will felt more quickly than the rest of the fibre and recede away from the edge. Sometimes this happens before the embellishments are fully bonded, so they might start to poke up and, again, interfere with the top edge.

Overlapping materials

When we are felting embellishments to the wool fibre, they don't just end up lying on top of the finished felt, they actually become embedded. For this to happen, the wool fibre has to penetrate through and around all the embellishments to grab hold of them and pull them into the fibre itself. It makes it harder to achieve this if you have a thick layer of overlapping embellishments covering the entire ball. So avoid everything overlapping in the same place, and keep some clear space on the ball for the fibre to migrate through.

Keeping the embellishments wet

The longer and more detailed your layout, the more the embellishments will dry out. Keep spraying your embellishments throughout this stage to keep them wet, pressing them firmly with a wet and soapy hand to keep them flat and tight against the ball.

Heavy embellishments

If you have trickier or heavier embellishments which are in danger of peeling away from the ball during the initial layout stage (such as a spiral of yarn on the bottom), then you could add some of the layer one wool fibre immediately on top of those areas to secure them whilst you complete the rest of the embellishment design on another area of the ball. Also avoid placing the ball in the bowl vertically – a spiral on the bottom is likely to fall off due to gravity, but if you just tip the ball to one side there's less chance of this. Another tip is to use a very fine material on top which offers a wide amount of coverage and is a good sticker, like silk fibres/hankies/caps.

Laying Out the Wool Fibre

Using three layers

Generally, using more finer layers of fibre in felting rather than one big thick layer helps with the fibres bonding and with creating an even layout, as three layers will average out into one even layout overall. Three layers is also helpful for inserting structural additions in between, such as pockets. Occasionally I use four layers, particularly if using a cutaway resist technique between layers, to ensure the felt will be structurally thick enough. Some felting techniques advise you to rub the fibre in between layers, but I don't recommend this as there is a risk of the layers felting individually and then not bonding properly as a combined whole.

Layers consist of many small overlapping pieces

Bear in mind that each layer is made up of lots of smaller, slightly overlapping pieces. There are likely to be at least two thicknesses of those pieces all over the ball to create one combined layer.

Direction of fibre

Since we are using carded wool fibre for the majority of the projects, in which the individual fibres are all lying in different directions, the direction of the pieces does not matter.

Wispy fibre edges

Keep the edges of each piece of fibre as wispy as possible for better integration.

Keeping the top edge wispy

Although you are laying out your fibre up to your chosen top edge, you do not need to be precise because you are going to fold over the edge later to neaten and thicken it. So go over the edge line with wispy fibre, which will make it easier to fold over. The same applies to the top of pockets.

Don't add all the fibre of one colour in one go

For each layer, aim to get just one piece's thickness-worth of fibre all over the ball first (a first 'pass'), in your chosen colour layout, then do a second pass over the ball with the remaining fibre to complete the layer, infilling the thinner areas. This way you'll find that you don't put too much fibre unevenly in one area, leaving another area too thin. This also helps you to adjust where a colour change might go if you find you have more of one colour remaining than another after the first pass on the ball. It further helps with protecting the embellishments to get at least one piece's thickness of fibre on top as quickly as you can to secure them in place.

Changing colour mid layer

When changing fibre colour during a layer, avoid butting up the two different colours next to each other at the colour change, as this could lead to a trench or thin area developing. Maintain the same process of overlapping wispy edges of fibre pieces as if they were the same colour, which will help to avoid thin areas developing and also create a more blended colour change.

Colour mixing

If you use a different colour for each fibre layer it helps with laying out the fibre evenly because you can see where you still need to place it. This also helps you to spot thinner areas. But the downside might be that the colours of the layers will all mix together, which might not be the look you are after. So to keep the outer colours of an item truer and stronger you can either use the same colour for all three layers (which you'd definitely want to do if you were aiming for a pure white or black result for instance), or, to make the layout a bit easier, often I use the same combination for layers one and two to give those colours some strength, with a different colour for layer three. I like to ensure that layer three is a good consistent final layer, so

I might also use a little more fibre. Another option to reduce colour mixing is to use different but similar colours for each layer, which helps you with the even layout but creates more of a subtle blend.

Keeping track of the fibre

If you're struggling to see where you have or haven't laid fibre when you're using the same or similar colours for individual layers, then patting the fibre is a good indicator of the thickness. Other techniques to help you keep track are to work logically around the ball, using the A–D placement markings as a guide, or to use a spare length of yarn to mark where you start and finish the layout or to divide the ball up into areas where you have and haven't already added fibre.

Using yarn to keep track of fibre placement during a solid colour layer.

Using more fibre

Patting the wool fibre during layout helps you to check for thin areas. If anywhere feels a little thin but you've used up your fibre allocation, or you've used it up and haven't completed the full layer, just add more. The amounts listed in the projects are the minimums to ensure a good structural result, but adding more will make little difference to the end result.

Using larger fibre pieces

Wool fibre stretches once wet, which is why I recommend tearing your fibre into palm-sized pieces to make it manageable. But if you are comfortable using bigger than palm-sized pieces then that's totally fine, just continue to smooth down the edges and aim for an integrated layout from your pieces.

Keep emptying the propping-up bowl

As fast as we are putting water into the fibre, it is dripping out into the bowl beneath the ball. Keep emptying this water back into the main water bowl to avoid it developing a suction and pulling fibre off the bottom of the ball.

Using plastic to hold the fibre

If your fibre is drying out very quickly and peeling off, try using a piece of plastic to hold it in place until you've completed the whole layout. Spray the fibre in the area, place a large piece of plastic on top and then place the ball onto the propping-up bowl so that the plastic is tightly held by the edges of the bowl. That will keep everything in place whilst you work on a different area of the ball.

Rubbing the Fibre

Covering the fibre with thin plastic

I've started doing this more recently and have found it really successful as a way to keep the fibre in place better initially, with less disruption when putting the ball in the tights. It also removes the possibility of the tights felting to the fibre and reduces potential ball slippage within the fibre, as the plastic holds the ball in place at the top opening. On the whole it keeps water trapped inside the plastic and therefore within the fibre better, although the downside is that it stops additional water getting in. So when you peel back the plastic at any time between rounds, and especially after the first round, check the fibre for dryness and add extra soapy water. I tend to leave the plastic on until the end of the bouncing stage to help retain as much water as possible. You don't need to completely remove the plastic after each round, just peel back enough to reveal the edge or whichever part you need to check.

Push rubs

You might wonder why each round has 400 push rubs. The reason for this is that it is just long enough to make a difference to the fibre's development, but not long enough that if there is a problem we have left it too late to resolve, because the fibre is too felted. Folding over the top edge after the first round is a good example. The first round gives us just long enough for the fibres to start bonding, so that the edge is firm enough to fold neatly. But the fibre is not so bonded that we can't get the edge folds to join and bond. (NB: Before I started covering the fibre in plastic I used four rounds of 300 push rubs, so the same 1,200 in total but in more rounds. This was mainly to avoid the tights felting to the fibre. As the plastic removes this problem, I've changed the basic recipe so that there are less rounds and unwrapping.)

Start gently

When the fibre is initially wet and soapy it is mouldable, which is handy for making shapes like a flap. But it also means it still has the potential to move around, until the point when it has firmed up a bit. So go gently at the start of the push rubs to ensure you don't inadvertently start moving the fibre around and creating thin areas.

Ball slippage

Another reason for starting gently is that sometimes the ball and fibre can become disconnected and the ball slips around within the fibre shape. It isn't a problem if it happens later in the process once the fibre and embellishments have had time to bond, but if it happens during the early push rub rounds then there is a danger that the ball has moved with the embellishments, which might mean that your surface design is displaced. I've found this to be more of a problem when using smaller balls within a larger bowl during push rubs, which I think is down to moving the ball around too fast. Using a plastic layer, snug tights and a snug bowl will help reduce the risk of this happening.

Example of slippage of the medium green ball inside a prefelt bag shape.

Adding more fibre

The more felted the fibre, the harder it is to add more fibre if you need to, such as to cover a thin area. This is because the scales of the original fibres have already opened, locked together and are closing, thus developing a 'skin', which makes it hard for a new set of fibre scales to bond with them. So ideally you would complete all your layout at the same time. But if you start felting and find a thin area, the quicker you try to add extra fibre, the more success you are likely to have in getting it to bond. Generally I find that adding one larger piece of new fibre to cover the problem area is more likely to adhere than several smaller pieces, as there are less edges to felt in. Dunk and place your new larger piece and give it a gentle rub through the plastic for a few minutes to encourage it to bond, and then go back to the push rubs, and keep checking and rubbing it between rounds.

Checking the fibre between rounds

The reason we keep checking the fibre is that one round gives enough time for the fibre to make progress but not so far that we can't still make adjustments if we need to. Checking also enables us to add more soapy water directly to the fibre if needed. Having distinct rounds also makes it easier to complete the stages as it provides stopping points (and breaks!) between each one. The upshot is that it is better to take your time to keep checking what the fibre needs at any given stage, and adjusting accordingly, rather than motoring through the felting process and then having to deal with problems at the end.

Bouncing the Fibre
Slack fibre

You might notice during bouncing that the fibre area which has been making contact with your work surface goes slightly

Rubbing slack fibre smooth after bouncing.

slack or wrinkled, particularly on projects which have a wider opening (like a basket) as the fibre is less constrained by the ball. This is down to the impact of the bouncing, so just give the slack area a rub to tighten it back up against the ball.

Fulling the Fibre

Rubbing the embellishments

Once you remove the ball from the prefelt you can finally see how well any embellishments have bonded to the fibre. Run your fingers across any embellishments in a counter direction to check whether they are still moving. If not, move on to throwing the prefelt. If there is still movement, spend a few minutes rubbing them with very soapy hands (also give the inside a soapy shower first) to bond them in place. The key to rubbing is not to move the embellishments as you rub, to avoid displacing them. Think of your hand like an electric sander, hold it firmly on top of the embellishments and vibrate your hand more than move it. Rub in this way around the whole of the inside before starting to throw and continue to rub after every 50 throws initially to help the bonding. You can move your hand more as you rub once the embellishments feel bonded in place, always in the direction that the embellishments are laid rather than across them. I like to use olive oil soap for hands-on rubbing of the embellishments as its thick and sticky consistency helps to stick them in place slightly before you start throwing, which helps their overall bonding with the fibre.

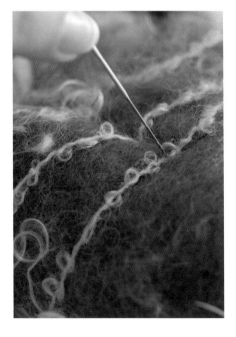

Needle felting a loose yarn at prefelt stage.

Making adjustments

If you remove the ball and find that there are areas of your project you are not happy with (such as a strand of yarn which has strayed too far up) or aspects which need remedial action (such as a small hole in the fibre), then the prefelt stage is the right time to address these issues. It is always better to make any adjustments, like cutting or picking away surface design elements you don't like, needle felting a loose yarn or some extra fibre over a thin area or hole, or adding a few stitches to some fabric which hasn't adhered fully, at this stage as it is still early enough for us to disguise them. Make your changes, give the changed areas a good soapy rub and then carry on the fulling process. Shrinking is the next stage, which changes the whole look of the surface as well as the size and shape of the felt, so you're very unlikely to notice any of those amendments by the end.

Soaking before throwing

As a lot of water will have been lost through the bouncing, give the whole prefelt a soak in fresh, very warm, soapy water before throwing. The prefelt needs the water, the extra weight helps make the throwing more effective and the heat will help with shrinkage.

Fibre shedding

This often occurs during fulling/shaping when you are rubbing the fibres directly with your hands and it causes the wool to pill (when the fibres collect up into small balls on the surface) and leave fibres on your hands. This happens naturally when rubbing wool fibres. Once you've stopped rubbing and have rinsed, it stops and doesn't cause a lasting problem.

Removing surface wrinkles

If you're not keen on natural wrinkles, then you need to spend time during the fulling/shaping stage to stretch them out and rub the felt smooth.

Finishing the Felt

Creating a smooth finished surface

Inserting the felting ball after rinsing is a good use of a finishing forma to both shape the finished felt and stretch out the surface. If you're aiming for a different shape, try and find another household item you can use, or firmly pack your shape with bubble wrap or a towel.

CHAPTER 3

FELTING SIMPLE 3D FORMS

ow that we've gone through the basic process of felting on a ball in detail in the previous chapter, to create a simple bowl embellished with wool yarns and other fibres, we can move on to try out some different shapes and embellishment materials. The projects in this chapter are all straightforward to create, but each has a challenge in terms of either the materials used, getting the sizing right or covering more of the ball with fibre. As always, bear in mind that you can mix and match any of the techniques and projects. We're going to start with another type of vessel, but this one is quite different to the sample bowl in the previous chapter.

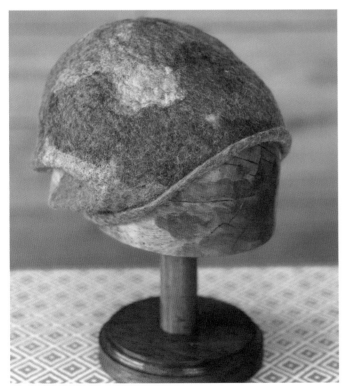

Slouchy hat variation using Maori-Bergschaf carded wool batt fibre and silk fibres.

Small cushion variation using Bergschaf carded wool batt fibre, silk fibres and chunky thick and thin wool yarn.

COILED ROPE VESSEL PROJECT

Our first project is a small decorative vessel, more like a vase than a bowl, using New Zealand carded wool fibre and chunky wool yarns to create a coiled rope effect. The tight coiling of variegated yarns on the surface creates incredible patterns as the fibre behind it shrinks. This is a relatively quick project because we're using the small blue ball, a simple fibre layout and just one type of embellishment.

You might be wondering what you can learn from this project, which surely looks easier (as it is smaller) and simpler (as there is only one type of embellishment) than the Embellished Bowl Sample Project in Chapter 2. The big difference here is the type of yarns we're using and the tight coiling technique. Unlike mohair yarns, which are relatively lightweight plus hairy so they expand and grip on the ball more easily, these chunky wool yarns become quite heavy when wet, which increases the risk of them falling off the ball during the layout stage. So that's the first challenge, which we'll address by working on the layout in two halves. The second challenge is that the tight coiling of yarns creates a thick outer top layer, which makes it harder for the wool fibre to migrate through to the front to grab the yarns and embed them. This means that we need to do extra rubbing of the surface, both inside and out, to ensure the yarns are completely secure. But I feel that those extra challenges are worth it when you see the organic wavy yarn design which results from the yarns shrinking as a collective layer.

You can use any kind of chunky wool yarns, although variegated ones will give the most striking colour effects. I've used thick and thin yarn which varies in thickness. This means that sometimes the shape dips down in areas where lots of thin parts are next to each other, or raises up where lots of thick parts are next to each other. Generally the coiling evens out to the same height in the end, but if not you can always push the yarns down to squeeze them together, or add in extra pieces of yarn to raise up lower areas. Chunky yarns of an even thickness will create a slightly different look, as will coiling the yarns more loosely around the ball, leaving gaps in between.

It's worth noting that, because they are so thick and create such a substantial surface layer, the yarns contribute just as much to the weight and structure of the vessel as the wool fibre (the fibre weighs 40g and the yarn 32g). So I've treated them as a replacement for the first layer of fibre and only used two fibre layers for this project. Also, as you don't see much of the fibre on the finished surface, I've just used two plain colours in a solid separate colour layer each, for ease of layout.

WHAT YOU WILL NEED

Materials
- Approximately 40g of carded wool fibre in your chosen colours: 20g per main layer (×2)
- I used New Zealand carded wool batt fibre in the following combination:

Layout Element	Colour	Amount
Layer 1	Purple	20g
Layer 2	Spring green	20g

- Approximately 15m (32g) of variegated colour thick and thin chunky wool yarns (I used two types: a darker one in the bottom half and a brighter one in the top half)

Equipment
- Small blue ball, inflated to 51cm (20in) circumference
- Inflating pump with valve
- Small round bowl to prop up the ball
- Large bowl of any size to hold the washing-up liquid and warm water solution
- 25cm (10in) internal diameter round bowl or similar (to push rub the ball within)
- One pair of small/medium (86–102cm/34–40in hips) tights/pantyhose, 20 denier (see Chapter 1 for preparation)
- 75cm × 30cm (30in × 12in) piece of thin plastic
- Washing-up/dishwashing liquid
- Olive oil soap
- Spray bottle (containing washing-up liquid and warm water solution)
- Ball brause
- Several large towels
- Several small/tea towels
- Scales
- Tape measure
- Small scissors

Bear in mind when you've removed the ball that the thick yarn layer will retain a concave shape, so it's a good idea to turn the vessel the right side out earlier than normal to correct this before it's fully felted, therefore turning the yarn layer from concave to convex. Because we are using a small amount of fibre on a small layout, the whole felting process will happen quickly so keep an eye on changes in the fibre.

I've included a few different variations after the main project, showing the same coiled rope technique at the same ball starting size and fibre weights but with different layouts and shaping. I've also shown what you can do with a bigger version to create a large coiled rope dish.

The finished vessel weighs approximately 72g and measures approximately 14cm wide × 15cm high × 8cm deep (5.5in × 6in × 3in).

Step by Step

Step 1: Assembling and preparing your materials

Collect your carded wool fibre and chunky wool yarns together to create a pleasing colour palette. Weigh 20g of fibre in your chosen colours for each of the two layers. Tear all fibre into palm-sized pieces. Inflate the small blue felting ball to 51cm (20in) in circumference and place it upside down on the propping-up bowl.

Step 2: Adding the first chunky yarn

Take the first yarn, unwind at least 1m (40in) and dunk it in soapy water, without cutting it and keeping hold of the loose end. Starting with the loose end, coil the yarn onto the ball in a tight spiral from the centre bottom point going around the ball right down to the middle design line. Unwind and soak more yarn as needed, then cut off.

Step 3: Layer one initial fibre layout

Using 5–10g of the 20g fibre allocation for layer one, take a piece of the purple fibre, dunk it in soapy water, ensure it is spread out and completely soaked and place it directly on top of the coiled yarn. Repeat to cover all the coiled yarn layout from the base to the middle design line with a single thickness of fibre.

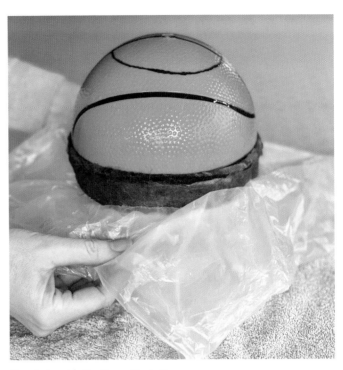

Step 4: Covering the fibre with plastic

Cover the fibre with a piece of plastic. Turn the ball right side up and place it back on the propping-up bowl so that the sides of the bowl hold the plastic (and therefore also the fibre and yarns) in place. Peel back the plastic at the middle design line, and any fibre just covering the yarn, so that you can access the end of the coil.

Step 5: Adding the second chunky yarn

Repeat Step 2 to add the second chunky yarn to the ball. Starting where the first yarn ended, continue to coil the yarn tightly around the ball right up to the top circle line. If the design dips as you coil, you could cut and move thicker yarn areas to raise up lower parts of the design or insert extra lengths of yarn.

Step 6: Completing layer one fibre layout

Repeat Step 3 with some of the remaining layer one fibre to cover the yarn from the middle design line up to the top circle line. Then remove the plastic and go over the ball again, creating as even a fibre layer as possible and infilling thinner areas until all the layer one fibre is used.

Step 7: Completing layer two fibre layout

Take the green layer two fibre allocation and repeat the dunk and place method to add all the fibre allocation to the ball, in as even a layer as possible. Add any extra fibre you feel necessary to thicken thin areas. Generously spray the fibre all over and wrap in plastic.

Step 8: Preparing to rub the fibre

Stretch one pair of tights over the 25cm (10in) internal diameter round bowl, place the ball inside and gently pull up the edges of the tights as high as they will go. If the ball is completely enclosed in the tights, tie a loose knot in the top to secure. If not, place the ball in a second pair to cover the area not covered by the first pair.

Step 9: Rubbing the fibre

Place the ball inside the bowl, pour on soapy water to ensure the whole ball and tights are soaked, and gently push the ball around the bowl in all directions, ensuring that the ball makes contact with the sides of the bowl but not pushing so hard that the fibres are moved out of place. Repeat the pushing/rubbing action for 400 pushes.

Step 10: Neatening the top edge

Peel the tights away from the ball and back over the edges of the bowl, and place the ball on the propping-up bowl. Peel back the plastic to reveal the top opening edge of the fibre. Neaten the edge all around by fluffing it up, folding it outwards, spraying and gently rubbing. Replace the plastic and tights.

Step 11: Completing the rubbing

Repeat the push rub action for 400 pushes twice more, making 1,200 pushes in total, pushing more firmly each time. Remove the ball from the tights/plastic after each round, add more soapy water if the fibre seems dry at any point and spray and rub the top edge to ensure integration with the main fibre.

Step 12: Bouncing the ball

Place the ball in the tights and bounce it on your work surface 500 times. The easiest method is to hold the tights above the ball whilst bouncing. After 500 bounces, remove the tights/plastic to check/rub the top edge as before. Repeat this process at least once more, alternating ball placement in the tights each time.

Step 13: Removing the ball

The fibre around the ball should now feel much firmer, tighter and thicker. If not, replace the tights and complete a further round of 500 bounces or more until the fibre is feeling more solid and fully integrated with itself. Remove the tights and plastic, deflate the ball and remove it from the prefelt vessel shape.

Step 14: Rubbing the wool yarns

Carefully turn the vessel right side out, soak it in warm soapy water and spend some time firmly rubbing the yarns, in the direction they are laid in, to fully bond them with the wool fibre. Check they are partly adhered before turning, otherwise rub the yarns from inside and only turn right side out to rub when they are already partly secure.

Step 15: Throwing the vessel

Turn the vessel back to the wrong side out. Loosely pick it up and throw it on the work surface 100 times, spinning it around on its sides as you throw and maintaining the rounded shape. After 100 throws, reshape it and rub the yarns on the inside to continue to encourage them to bond to the fibre. Repeat for a further 200 throws.

Step 16: Shaping the vessel

Turn the vessel back to the right side out and continue to shape and shrink it using an alternating combination of techniques: throwing it, rubbing the yarns, stretching with your hands inside (to change from a rounded to flatter profile shape) and flattening the base. Stop when the vessel is able to keep an upright structure.

Step 17: Finishing the vessel

Rinse the vessel under warm running water, or soak in bowls of warm water, squeezing gently until the water runs clear. Alternate between warm- and cold-water rinses if the felt still needs firming. Remove excess water by rolling the vessel up in a dry towel, then reshape and leave to air dry on a towel.

ROUNDED COILED ROPE VESSEL

For the first variation I wanted to highlight that you can make your finished items look quite different through small tweaks to the layout and shaping. So for this vessel I largely repeated the main project, with the same measurements and weights, although I used Finnwool carded wool batt fibre (again with purple for layer one, but a dark grey for layer two) and a slightly different chunky thick and thin wool yarn. The main differences are:

- I raised up the top edge of the vessel to create a smaller opening, so instead of using the marked 10cm (4in) diameter top circle line I laid out the yarns and fibre to leave a 7.5cm (3in) diameter circle opening.
- I shaped the vessel differently during fulling, encouraging the rounded shape rather than flattening it into more of an upside-down triangle shape as I did for the main version. The opening hole was much smaller but was just big enough to still get my hand inside. As the finished item was so sturdy I didn't feel it needed stretching or shaping around a forma. If I had wanted to, the opening was too small to reinsert the ball but I could have stuffed it with bubble wrap.

Coiled rope vessel technique, starting from the base.

Coiled rope vessel technique, up to a 7.5cm (3in) diameter opening.

PART COILED ROPE VESSEL

This is a further variation on the coiled rope technique, showing a part yarn design going in a different direction as well as illustrating how a finishing forma can help you achieve a different vessel shape from the same prefelt starting point. The measurements and opening circle size were again the same as for the main project, although I used 40g of variegated Corriedale carded wool sliver fibre in a mix of turquoise and lilac shades for each of the two layers.

The main challenge was keeping the chunky yarn on the ball during layout, because it wanted to fall off due to its weight and gravity-defying position. So this is where it helps to work in stages, covering each portion in fibre and plastic before moving to the next area.

The other key difference here is in how I shaped the vessel. This time, after removing the ball, turning the prefelt right side out and rubbing the yarns, I inserted the tin finishing forma (covered in clingfilm to protect it) to do some initial shaping. This included pulling the fibre upwards to create a smaller base and taller, narrower sides. With the tin still inside, I then alternated throwing with rubbing the fibre around the tin, causing the prefelt to shrink and take on the shape of the forma. I stopped fulling whilst the felt was slightly loose around the tin, so that after rinsing I could still re-insert it and leave it to dry inside.

Part coiled rope technique vessel during yarn layout around the middle design line.

Finished part coiled rope vessel with finishing forma tin.

COILED ROPE DISH

The final variation uses the coiled rope technique at a much larger size and with both the yarn and fibre only going up to the middle design line. The fibre therefore stops at the widest point of the ball, so that when we remove it we have a very wide and shallow dish shape. The advantage of using the coiled rope technique is that the yarn adds structure to the finished dish, helping to keep the concave shape because it has not only felted to the fibre but also to itself, in the same position as if it were still on the ball. I placed it on a similar-sized china dish as a finishing forma whilst it dried but I think it would have kept its shape even if I hadn't. Here are some of the key measurements and details of how I made this:

- I used the large purple felting ball at 89cm (35in) in circumference.
- I used a mix of chunky thick and thin yarns in the centre and straight chunky yarns further out, in a rainbow selection and amounting to approximately 35g. The coil was slightly looser than the previous projects. You can see on the finished dish how the central thick and thin yarns have created more of a wiggly pattern than the straight outer yarns.
- I used approximately 70g of New Zealand carded wool batt fibre in total, in green (10g), turquoise (14g), purple (20g) and pink (25g) shades. To keep the corresponding yarn colours truer, in the layer one and two layouts I used a circle of green fibre in the centre, 15cm (6in) in diameter, then 15cm (6in) bands of blue and purple further outwards. I used a solid layer of magenta pink in layer three.

- I followed the usual felting process before removing the prefelt dish from the ball. As before, I needed to do a lot of extra rubbing to ensure the yarns were fully adhered. Then I was very careful during the fulling stage to alternate between flipping the dish over front and back whilst throwing, and moulding it with my hands, to not flatten it completely and still maintain the concave dish shape.
- The finished dish weighs approximately 107g and measures approximately 26.5cm in diameter × 7.5cm high (10.5in × 3in).

New Zealand fibre and mix of chunky wool yarns to create the coiled rope dish.

Initial yarn layout for the coiled rope dish, from the base to the middle design line.

Layers one and two fibre layout for the coiled rope dish, in bands of colour.

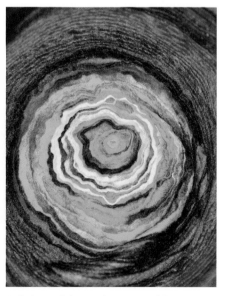

Coiled rope dish yarn design at prefelt stage.

Finished coiled rope dish left to dry on a china dish finishing forma.

SLOUCHY HAT PROJECT

I'm a big fan of a knitted or crocheted slouchy hat, so here is my take on a wet felted version. This isn't a true slouchy hat because it still has structure to it and holds its shape, so the drape/slouchiness at the back of the hat is permanently shaped rather than loose. But I've deliberately chosen a wool fibre which retains its softness and flexibility even when well felted. As the total weight is only 100g, it is a comfortable shape and weight to wear, feeling more like a thick knitted hat than stiff felt, as well as being quick to felt.

This is a relatively straightforward project with a simple and quick embellishment and fibre layout. I've used viscose fibres as the surface design layer, to give a gentle variegation, on top of a Maori-Bergschaf carded wool batt fibre mix, which is well suited to a soft hat project where you might not want a rigid result. The Maori-Bergschaf colour range comprises a subtle blend, and I've also been very conservative with my colours (using two similar purple/lilac shades) to make this a very wearable hat for autumn/winter, but you could go much brighter with both the wool and viscose fibres to make the latter really stand out.

As the viscose fibres are so delicate and wispy, this is a project where adding the fibres dry onto the wet ball and spraying is the most successful way of controlling the layout. Once wet, they'll stay in place quite well until you're ready to secure them with wool fibre. But if you're struggling with your fibres moving, you could complete the layout in sections and then add a few pieces of wool fibre on top to protect them whilst you work on another area.

The main challenge with a hat project is getting the opening size right so that it fits your head. The two key measurements to get right are:

- Your own head size. I've based the project measurements on my head size, measured at an angle from the back of my head, covering my ears, to my forehead, which is where the hat will sit, which for me is approximately 55cm (21.5in). If your head is bigger than this then add a corresponding 2–3cm (0.5–1in) to the starting ball circumference for every 2–3cm (0.5–1in) bigger your head is (or reduce it similarly for a smaller size).
- The target end size. These are the measurements to aim for when you need to stop felting so that the hat doesn't shrink too far. Sizes are shown in Steps 13, 16 and 19, but if you change the starting ball size then don't forget to add (or subtract) the same amount to the target sizes.

Materials

- Approximately 90g of carded wool fibre in your chosen colours: 30g per main layer (×3)
- I used Maori-Bergschaf carded wool batt fibre in the following combination:

Layout Element	Colour	Amount
Layer 1	Purple	30g
Layer 2	Purple	30g
Layer 2	Lilac	30g

- Approximately 15g of embellishment fibres (I used viscose tops in three shades of purple/lilac/dusky pink, 5g of each)

Equipment

- Large purple felting ball, inflated to 80cm (31.5in) circumference
- Green felting ball, inflatable to 74cm (29in) circumference
- Inflating pump
- Small round bowl to prop up the ball
- Large bowl of any size to hold the washing-up liquid and warm water solution
- 28cm (11in) minimum internal diameter round or square bowl (to push rub the ball within)
- Two pairs of medium/large (102–122cm/40–48in hips) tights/pantyhose, 20 denier (see Chapter 1 for preparation)
- 100cm × 55cm (40in × 22in) piece of thin plastic
- Washing-up/dishwashing liquid
- Olive oil soap
- Spray bottle (containing washing-up liquid and warm water solution)
- Ball brause
- Several large towels
- Several small/tea towels
- Scales
- Tape measure
- Small scissors

You don't need to worry about any other measurements as there is lots of room in the main body of the hat (which we need in order to create the slouchy element), so our focus is on getting the opening size right. Inflating a ball inside the hat after rinsing as a finishing forma also ensures we are stretching the hat (but not the opening) to give us plenty of hat to work with, in addition to smoothing the surface and ensuring a rounded shape.

Fortunately we also have some size tolerance in felting during the shrinkage stage, so we can easily make further adjustments to get it right for your head. In order to retain a larger size, we can stop felting sooner and/or deliberately stretch the opening throughout the fulling process, so regularly check the size throughout. You'll notice that the initial opening size when we remove the ball is smaller than the end size, because we are stretching it to straighten it (Step 15) and folding the edge up slightly (Step 18).

You can use any wool fibre or embellishments you prefer, but be aware that the challenge of felting to an exact end size means that there is always a risk of needing to overfelt the fibre to get the size down, which might mean that your surface design sinks further into the fibre and disappears, or underfelting it because you've reached the target size and your embellishments might not have felted in fully. I found that the Maori-Bergschaf is quite a slow felter, so I completed around 300 throws after removing the ball to reach the target size, which meant that the wool fibre ate up the viscose embellishment and a lot of the wool's hairiness came through. So it is always worth making a test with the exact wool fibre and embellishments you want to use to see if you get the finished effect you want.

If you're not keen on a slouchy hat, there is an alternative version shown in the Sari Silk Hat Variation Project in Chapter 5, which uses exactly the same process and instructions but is shaped differently at the end, so you might like that instead. This is the sort of project where you can shape the hat as you like so you've got scope to make changes from the same basic design.

The finished hat weighs approximately 100g and measures approximately 23cm wide × 17cm high (9in × 6.75in), with an opening size of 56cm (22in).

Step by Step

Step 1: Assembling and preparing your materials

Collect your carded wool fibre and viscose tops together to create a pleasing colour palette. Weigh 30g of wool fibre in your chosen colours for each of the three layers. Tear all fibre into palm-sized pieces. Inflate the felting ball to 80cm (31.5in) in circumference.

Step 2: Adding the first colour of embellishment fibres

With the felting ball upside down on the propping-up bowl, spray the surface to help the viscose fibres stick. Working on an accessible area of the ball, take a wisp of the first fibre colour and place on the ball, then add five or six more wisps in random positions and directions. Spray to secure in place.

Step 3: Adding other colours of embellishment fibres

Working on the same accessible area of the ball, repeat Step 2 with your second viscose fibre colour to add more wisps on the ball, varying the direction and placement and overlapping the first fibre colour in places. Then repeat Step 2 for the third colour of viscose fibres until you have built up a solid layer of overlapping fibres.

Step 4: Completing the embellishment fibre layout

Once you're happy with the overall fibre coverage on one area of the ball, move the ball position to access another area and repeat Steps 2 and 3. Continue laying out embellishment fibres on the ball in this way until the entire ball is covered except the top circle opening (the wisps should overlap the top circle line). Spray to secure.

Step 5: Layer one fibre layout

Using the 30g fibre allocation for layer one, take a piece of the purple fibre, dunk it in soapy water, ensure it is spread out and completely soaked and place it directly on top of the fibres anywhere on the ball. Repeat to cover the whole ball up to the top circle line. Infill any thinner areas until you have used all the layer one fibre.

Step 6: Finishing layers two and three fibre layout

Repeat the dunk and place method outlined in Step 5 with the layer two (purple) and layer three (lilac) 30g fibre allocations. Pat regularly to check evenness, smooth the fibres down with soapy hands and add any extra fibre you feel necessary to thicken thin areas. Generously spray the fibre all over and wrap in plastic.

Step 7: Preparing to rub the fibre

Stretch one pair of tights over the 28cm (11in) internal diameter rubbing bowl, place the ball inside with the plug facing downwards and gently pull up the edges of the tights as high as they will go. Repeat with the second pair of tights, this time placing the ball inside so that the area not covered by the first pair is covered.

Step 8: Rubbing the fibre

Place the ball inside the bowl, pour on soapy water to ensure the whole ball and tights are soaked, and gently push the ball around the bowl in all directions, ensuring that the ball makes contact with the sides of the bowl but not pushing so hard that the fibres are moved out of place. Repeat the pushing/rubbing action for 400 pushes.

Step 9: Neatening the top edge

Peel each pair of tights away from the ball and back over the edges of the bowl, and place the ball on the propping-up bowl. Peel back the plastic to reveal the top edge of the fibre. Neaten it all around by fluffing up the wool/viscose edge, folding it outwards, spraying and gently rubbing. Trim the viscose fibre to neaten if necessary.

Step 10: Completing the rubbing

Replace the plastic and tights and repeat the push rub action for 400 pushes twice more, pushing more firmly each time. Remove the ball from the tights after each round and peel back the plastic to check the top edge fold is bonding to the rest of the fibre. Rub and smooth the edge/fibre and add soapy water as necessary.

Step 11: Bouncing the ball

Place the ball in the tights and bounce it on your work surface 500 times. The easiest method is to hold the tights above the ball whilst bouncing. After 500 bounces, remove the tights/plastic to check/rub the edges as before. Repeat this process twice more, alternating ball placement in the tights each time.

Step 12: Removing the ball

The fibre around the ball should now feel much firmer, tighter and thicker. If it has started to significantly recede away from the top edge, stop bouncing now. If not, complete a further round of 500 bounces, to make 2,000 in total. Then remove the tights and plastic, deflate the ball and remove it from the prefelt hat shape.

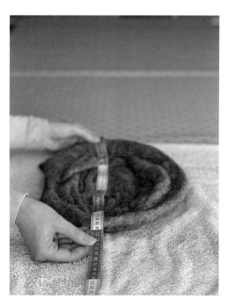

Step 13: Measuring the hat

Note the hat's flat measurements to help you check its progress as it shrinks during fulling. It will currently measure approximately 39cm across at its widest point × 33cm high × 25.5cm across the opening (15.5in × 13in × 10in). Note that the target size to stop fulling before rinsing is no less than 33cm × 28cm × 28cm (13in × 11in × 11in).

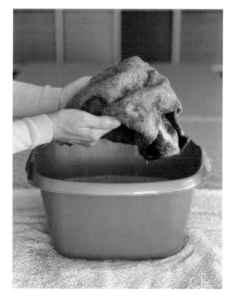

Step 14: Soaking the fibre

Check the viscose fibres are well bonded on the inside and not moving. If they are (or you are using embellishments other than fine tops fibres), give the inside a good soapy shower and rub the inside until the fibres/embellishments are staying firmly in place. Then dunk the felt completely in warm soapy water and gently squeeze.

Step 15: Straightening the opening edge

Flatten the hat and straighten the bottom opening edge, which will have a slight curve downwards at each side. Straighten it by gently stretching it downwards in the middle, which will expand the width of the opening edge. Repeat this action as necessary throughout the fulling stage to maintain the straight bottom edge of the hat.

Step 16: Throwing the hat

Loosely pick up the hat and throw it on the work surface 100 times, spinning the hat around on its sides as you throw and maintaining the rounded shape at all times. After 100 throws, flatten it and check the size. Continue to throw and measure in this way until the hat reaches the target size: 33cm × 28cm × 28cm (13in × 11in × 11in).

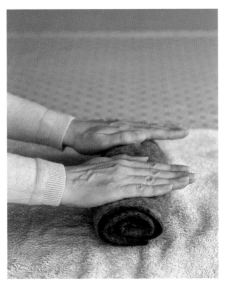

Step 17: Shrinking the hat

If your hat appears to be shrinking slowly, or has only reached one or two of the correct measurements, you could also target the shrinkage in a specific direction by rolling it on itself in the direction you need to shrink it. Roll for 25 rolls, check, and repeat as necessary. You could also try alternating hot and cold water rinses.

Step 18: Turning up the opening edge

Turn the hat viscose side out and fold up the bottom opening edge by approximately 1–1.5cm (0.5in). With soapy hands, rub repeatedly around the fold to encourage it to stay in position.

Step 19: Stretching the hat

Rinse the hat under warm running water, or soak in bowls of warm water, squeezing gently until the water runs clear. Remove excess water by rolling the hat up in a dry towel. Insert the green ball and inflate to 74cm (29in) circumference to stretch and smooth the hat's surface and effect a rounded shape. Deflate and remove the ball.

Step 20: Shaping the hat

Place the hat on your head with the opening on your forehead and smooth the hat down onto the back of your head. This will create a slouchy shape at the back, which will overhang the bottom edge at the back. Shape the overhang into two outward pleats, then remove the hat and adjust the pleats to neaten (*see* bamboo variation for example measurements).

Step 21: Finishing the hat

Once you are happy with the overall shape, leave the hat to air dry on a towel. You could stand it on a hat block if you have one, or use a smaller ball inflated to your head size to stand the hat on. Once dry, you could also steam iron the pleats to further define or reshape them as desired.

SLOUCHY HAT WITH BAMBOO

Here is another version of the slouchy hat, made with the same weights and measurements and also using Maori-Bergschaf carded wool batt fibre, but in blue and purple colours. The main difference is that I used bamboo tops fibre, in two plain blue and one variegated blue shade, instead of viscose. This is still a subtle embellishment layer, but although I did the same amount of throwing to full the hat after removing the ball (about 300 throws), the bamboo fibres seem to have stood their ground better than the viscose and are much more visible in the finished hat. As always, it shows how many variables there are in determining wet felting outcomes.

In terms of shaping the slouchy hat, there are multiple ways you could do this, but here are the approximate measurements for how I shaped both the main and variation project versions. First I created the lower outward pleat/fold approximately 10cm (4in) above the bottom edge, so that the pleat overhangs the bottom edge slightly. Then I made the second outward pleat/fold approximately 7cm (2.75in) above the first. A good tip is to try the hat on in front of a mirror and keep adjusting until you're happy with the look and fit.

Maori-Bergschaf carded wool fibre and bamboo tops embellishment used to create the blue slouchy hat.

Bamboo tops layout on the ball before adding the wool fibre.

Blue slouchy hat during the felting stage, with neatened top edge.

MANDALA CROCHET CUSHION PROJECT

Cushions offer a great way to showcase a bigger, more complete design as you have a whole side to display. As we're working on a sphere, we can use the felting on a ball technique to create a round cushion. Round cushion pads are available at a whole range of sizes, so you can make any size to suit you, as well as use any kind of surface design techniques. I've chosen to use a crocheted mandala design, as their round shape lends itself perfectly to this. You can find free and paid patterns online, as I have done for the banded star shape I've used, or you'll also find them in books, magazines and kits. If you're not a crocheter, then knitting or weaving with wool yarn would work equally well.

The key to making the design stand out is to make the structure of your crocheted piece quite loose and lacey, to account for the piece shrinking during felting, so I've increased the size of my crochet hook from both what the pattern and the yarn manufacturer recommend to accommodate this, so instead of 3mm I used a 6mm hook. I've used a hairy mohair blend yarn with some sparkle to it in five different colours. Just bear in mind that a thick and hairy mohair yarn will shrink up and hide the stitches more, whereas a finer yarn like kid silk mohair will show the individual design better. So there's scope for experimenting with different yarns, sizes and patterns to create different effects. You could also just lay out yarns on the ball to create a design instead, although a crocheted, knitted or woven piece will retain the pattern much more clearly.

Once you've made your yarn piece, the layout for this project is really quick as all you need to do is wet and place it on the ball before adding the wool fibre as usual. Fibre-wise, I used Bergschaf carded wool fibre in alternating layers of turquoise and orange, although I laid out orange in a small central circle on all the layers to keep the centre of the cushion pure orange rather than a mix. The layout is a bit different to other projects as we're orienting the felting ball quite differently. The base centre point and top centre plug, which are opposite each other, now mark the centres of each side of the cushion, and the usual middle design line now marks the narrow edge around the cushion. We're also covering the entire felting ball with fibre and creating a narrow flap overlap at the top centre plug, which will be the opening access to insert the cushion pad. (As this isn't a separate flap, but just an extension of the main layers, I'm including it in this chapter rather than Chapter 4.) I've chosen to close mine with magnetic clasp fasteners, but as an alternative in the first variation project I show you how to create a version with butted-up edges and a zip, which is simple to hand-sew in place. I added extra embellishment in the form of pompoms at the end of each star point, but this is totally optional!

And just a note about cushion pad sizes, which always seem to be sold in inches. I've found that these can be a bit variable. So the 11in and 13in cushion pads I used were sold respectively as 10in and 12in cushion pads. But the 20in pad really was 20in. Luckily we have wriggle room in felting and the beauty of using the cushion pad as a shaping/finishing forma means we can make the felt fit around the pad.

The finished cushion weighs approximately 660g with the pad and 325g without the pad. Without the pompoms, it measures approximately 74cm (29in) in circumference, 37cm (14.5in) in diameter. The cushion pad is 33cm (13in) in diameter. The finished opening is approximately 28cm (11in) wide.

Materials

- Approximately 165g of carded wool fibre in your chosen colours: 55g per main layer (×3)
- I used Bergschaf carded wool batt fibre in the following combination:

Layout Element	Colour	Amount
Layer 1	Turquoise	45g
Centre	Orange	7g
Flap	Turquoise	3g
Layer 2	Orange	52g
Flap	Orange	3g
Layer 3	Turquoise	45g
Centre	Orange	7g
Flap	Turquoise	3g

- Crocheted (or other technique) circular mandala piece measuring approximately 40.5cm (16in) in diameter when flat and 46cm (18in) in diameter when stretched. I used five colours of sparkly mohair yarn, in beige, yellow, orange, red and turquoise, up to a 50g (145m/159 yards) ball of each
- 4 × 50g (145m/159 yards) balls of the same yarn used to crochet the mandala to create 12 pompoms. I used four colours of sparkly mohair yarn, in yellow, orange, red and turquoise, up to a 50g ball of each
- 33cm (13in) (actual size) diameter round cushion pad (I used feather-filled)
- 3 × 14mm sew-on magnetic clasp fasteners
- Matching embroidery or sewing thread

Equipment

For the wet felting
- Large purple felting ball, inflated to 91.5cm (36in) circumference
- Inflating pump
- 36cm × 6cm (14in × 2.5in), 1–2mm thin foam or plastic resist template
- 25cm (10in) internal diameter round bowl or similar to prop up the ball
- Large bowl of any size to hold the washing-up liquid and warm water solution
- 32cm (12.5in) minimum internal diameter round or square bowl (to push rub the ball within)
- Two pairs of XXL (137–152cm/54-60in hips) tights/pantyhose, 20 denier (*see* Chapter 1 for preparation)
- 100cm × 55cm (40in × 22in) piece of thin plastic
- Large plastic bag
- Washing-up/dishwashing liquid
- Olive oil soap
- Spray bottle (containing washing-up liquid and warm water solution)
- Ball brause
- Several large towels
- Several small/tea towels
- Scales
- Tape measure
- Ruler
- Pen or pencil
- Small and large scissors

For finishing the cushion
- 6mm crochet hook
- Tape measure
- Pins
- Sewing needle
- Scissors
- 6.5mm (2.5in) pompom maker
- Large eye sewing needle

Step by Step

Step 1: Assembling and preparing your materials

Collect your carded wool fibre and completed yarn mandala together to create a pleasing colour palette. Weigh 55g of wool fibre in your chosen colours for each of the three layers, and from this keep 3g aside per layer to create the flap. Tear all fibre into palm-sized pieces. Inflate the felting ball to 91.5cm (36in) in circumference.

Step 2: Adding the mandala

With the base centre point facing up, place the ball on the propping-up bowl. Dunk the mandala in soapy water. Place it on the ball, with the right side (if it has one) facing the ball, oriented with the centre of the mandala placed exactly on the base centre point. Stretch the edges of the mandala to meet the middle design line.

Step 3: Layer one fibre layout

Using the main 52g fibre allocation for layer one (which I've divided into orange in the centre and turquoise everywhere else), take a piece of fibre, dunk it in soapy water, ensure it is spread out and completely soaked and place it directly on top of the mandala. Repeat to cover the mandala down to the middle design line.

Step 4: Continuing the layer one fibre layout

Turn the ball plug side up (cover the fibre in plastic before placing in the propping-up bowl, if preferred) and continue the fibre layout. Note that you will be completely covering the ball with fibre except leaving a thin 25.5cm (10in) opening along the dotted placement lines at A and C and extending to the top edge line each side.

Step 5: Finishing the layer one fibre layout

Go over the ball again, infilling thinner areas until all the layer one fibre is used. To prepare to add the flap fibre, wet and place the resist template onto the ball so that one long edge lies along the opening in the fibre and is touching the surface of the ball (apart from where it extends further onto the fibre each side).

Step 6: Adding the flap fibre

One fibre edge will now be covered by the template, leaving the other visible. Take the 3g fibre flap allocation for layer one and add it to the visible opening edge to extend the edge onto the template by approximately 5cm (2in), creating a flap. Keep the side edges of the flap straight.

Step 7: Layer two fibre layout

Repeat Steps 3–6 with the full 55g fibre allocation for layer two (I used orange), again using 3g for the layout on top of the flap. To access the fibre underneath the flap, gently lift and fold back the template. Ensure when you fold it back down that the upper long edge of the template is still touching the surface of the ball.

Step 8: Layer three fibre layout

Repeat Step 7 with the full 55g fibre allocation for layer three (I used turquoise with orange in the centre only again), using the same dunk and place fibre method and patting regularly to check evenness. Add any extra fibre you feel necessary to thicken thin areas.

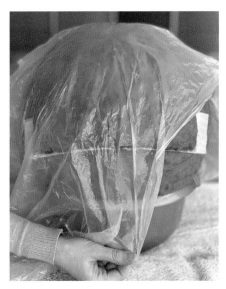

Step 9: Preparing to rub the fibre

Generously spray the fibre all over and wrap in plastic. Stretch one pair of tights over the 32cm (12.5in) internal diameter rubbing bowl, place the ball inside and gently pull up the edges of the tights as high as they will go. Repeat with the second pair of tights, placing the ball inside so that the area not covered by the first pair is covered.

Step 10: Rubbing the fibre

Place the ball inside the bowl, pour on soapy water to ensure the whole ball and tights are soaked, and gently push the ball around the bowl in all directions, ensuring that the ball makes contact with the sides of the bowl but not pushing so hard that the fibres are moved out of place. Repeat the pushing/rubbing action for 400 pushes.

Step 11: Neatening the flap

Peel each pair of tights away from the ball and back over the edges of the bowl, and place the ball on the propping-up bowl. Peel back the plastic to reveal the flap. Neaten the flap all around by fluffing up the edges, folding them outwards, spraying and gently rubbing. Then lift up the flap and neaten the other opening edge.

Step 12: Neatening under the flap

Remove the resist template and ensure that the join between the original top opening edge and the flap extension fibre is smooth and seamless: lift up any fibres which might still be stuck to the ball, spray with plenty of soapy water and smooth the join area with your hand. Replace the resist template and fold down the flap.

Step 13: Completing the rubbing

Replace the plastic and tights. Repeat the push rub action for 400 pushes twice more, pushing more firmly each time. Remove the ball from the tights/plastic after each round, spray and rub the flap edges and the lower opening edge underneath, then spray and smooth underneath the flap at the extension fibre join.

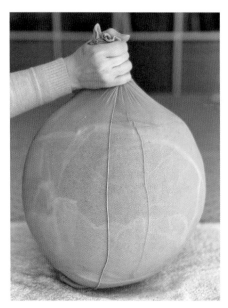

Step 14: Bouncing the ball

Place the ball in the tights and bounce it on your work surface 500 times. The easiest method is to hold the tights above the ball whilst bouncing. After 500 bounces, remove the tights/plastic/resist to check/rub the edges and flap join as before. Repeat this process at least three more times, alternating ball placement in the tights each time.

Step 15: Removing the ball

The fibre around the ball should now feel much firmer, tighter and thicker. If not, replace the tights and complete a further round of 500 bounces or more until the fibre is feeling more solid and fully integrated with itself. Remove the tights, plastic and resist, deflate the ball and remove it from the prefelt cushion shape.

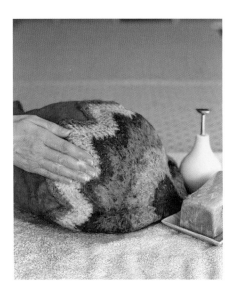

Step 16: Rubbing the mandala

Turn the cushion right side out and check whether the mandala has felted to the fibre by gently running your fingers across it. If it is not fully adhered, shower the fibre with soapy water in any loose areas and, with a very wet and soapy hand, do some focused rubbing (particularly around the mandala edges) until it stays firmly in place.

Step 17: Throwing the cushion

Turn the cushion inside out and give it a good soaking in warm soapy water. Then flatten it so that the two cushion sides are pushed together and throw it down onto the work surface 100 times, flipping it to the alternate side after every ten throws. This helps to set the shape of the cushion (two flat sides and a side edge all around).

Step 18: Shaping the cushion part 1

Put your hand inside the cushion and reshape it back to a fuller cushion shape. Stretch the flap edge to ensure a good overlap over the other opening edge, and neaten/straighten both edges by stretching and rubbing them into a pleasing shape. Repeat Steps 17 and 18 twice more, to make 300 throws, reshaping after each 100.

Step 19: Shaping the cushion part 2

If at any time during the 300 throws the flattened cushion starts to develop an oval shape, rather than round, roll it up on itself in the direction you want to shrink it and roll for ten rolls. This will have the effect of shrinking the cushion in that direction and enable you to maintain the round overall shape. Repeat as necessary.

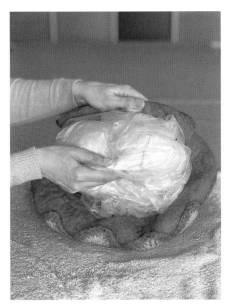

Step 20: Inserting the cushion pad

Turn the cushion right side out and insert the cushion pad (covered with a plastic bag to protect it from soap and water). Smooth and rub the cushion around the pad and stretch/adjust the flap and opening to ensure they are still neat and that the flap overlaps the opening.

Step 21: Shrinking the cushion to size

With the pad inside, repeat throwing the cushion approximately a further 200–300 times, flipping it on alternate sides every 20 throws and rubbing the cushion smooth all around after each round of 100. Also continue to check the opening edges and overlap, stretching and rubbing them to straighten as necessary.

Step 22: Rinsing the cushion

Once the cushion feels thick and sturdy and seems to fit comfortably around the pad, without being tight, remove the pad and rinse the cushion under warm running water, or soak in bowls of warm water, squeezing gently until the water runs clear. Remove excess water by rolling it up in a dry towel.

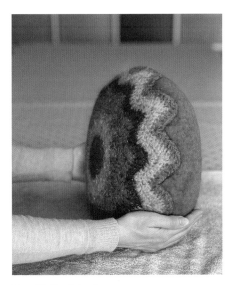

Step 23: Final shaping

Reshape the cushion and reinsert the cushion pad in a dry and clean plastic bag. Continue to rub and mould the cushion around the pad to create a smooth and rounded shape, and continue to neaten the flap and opening edge. Once happy with the overall shape, leave to air dry with the cushion pad still inside.

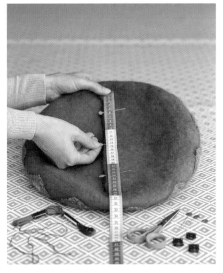

Step 24: Preparing to sew on the clasps

Once dry, remove the cushion pad. Steam iron the flap and opening to neaten and flatten them and decide whether you prefer the flap outside or tucked inside (I tucked mine inside). On whichever is now the upper, visible opening edge, measure and mark with pins the centre point and then two equal points each side.

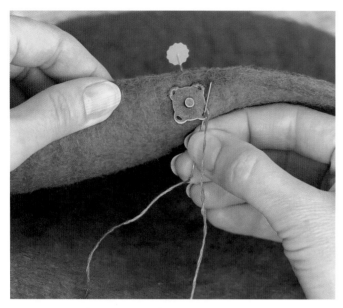

Step 25: Sewing the upper parts of the clasps

On the underside of the upper opening edge hand-sew one part of each magnetic clasp at each of the three marked points, approximately 5–10mm from the edge. Sew into the thickness of the felt, rather than going all the way through to the other side, to keep the stitches hidden on the outside. Reinsert the cushion pad.

Step 26: Sewing the lower parts of the clasps

Adjust/pull the upper opening edge across the lower opening edge until you are happy it looks neat and the cushion pad is hidden. Mark with pins the three points where the second part of each clasp needs to go on the lower opening edge (on top of the flap, in my case) and hand-sew each part to attach it.

Step 27: Making pompoms

Use a pompom maker to make 12 pompoms using the same yarns as used for the crochet mandala (I made three each of four colours). When securing the middle of each pompom, leave at least a 20cm (8in) length of yarn to enable you to attach them to the cushion. Trim each pompom as necessary to create a good ball shape.

Step 28: Attaching pompoms

Remove the cushion pad and hand-sew each pompom to the 12 outer points of the star, using the attached yarn to go right through to the inside of the cushion with your stitches and back out through the centre of each pompom at least twice to tightly secure them. Once complete, reinsert the cushion pad and match up the clasps.

SMALL SILK CLOUDS CUSHION

For the first variation I made a smaller cushion using silk fibres and a combination of wool fibres, along with a zip closure. Here are some key points to how I made this version:

- I used the large purple felting ball, inflated to 86.5cm (34in) in circumference.
- For the surface design, I used approximately 5g of hand-dyed silk fibres (bricks and hankies) in purple, blue and green shades, covering the base of the ball down to the middle design line. I cut off small pieces of the fibres, spread them apart with my fingers, placed them randomly on the ball and sprayed them to secure in place.
- For the fibre, I used approximately 120g in total, comprising a combination of hand-dyed Kent Romney combed wool tops for layer one (40g) in variegated shades of teals, purples and greens and, because I didn't have enough of it, 40g each of teal and purple New Zealand carded wool fibre for layers two and three. Using the carded wool helped to even out any possible unevenness from the tops layer.
- For the opening, I left a 23cm (9in) long thin gap in the fibre in a similar way to Step 4 of the main project. But, instead of adding a flap, I left the edges just butting up, and focused on keeping them butted up, stretching the edges as necessary throughout the felting process. The opening ended up the same length after felting. To finish the project, I hand-sewed a 40.5cm (16in) dark blue zip to the inside of the felt (*see* Chapter 7 for full details).

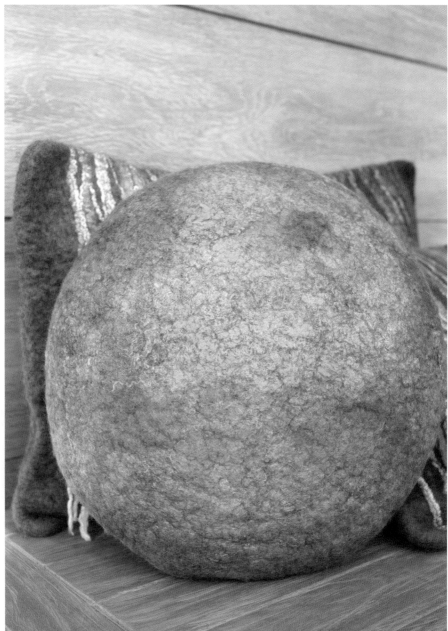

- The finished cushion measures approximately 63.5cm (25in) in circumference and I used a 28cm (11in) diameter (56cm/22in circumference) round feather cushion pad.

Mix of carded wool batt and combed tops, plus silk fibre embellishment, used to create the silk cushion.

Silk fibre layout on the ball, covering the base down to the middle design line.

Layer one wool fibre layout, using hand-dyed Kent Romney combed wool tops.

Layer three wool fibre layout, using New Zealand carded wool fibre.

Silk cushion reverse showing the hand-sewn zip closure.

MANDALA CROCHET POUFFE

For the second cushion variation project I've used the same crochet mandala design to create a large pouffe or footstool. The challenge here is felting something so large, because there's a lot of wet fibre to manage, but keeping the layout simple with the crocheted surface design and block colour fibre layers helps. Here are the main points to note:

- I used the extra large yellow ball, inflated to 117cm (46in) in circumference.
- I created the mandala using the same star pattern as the main project and approximately 90g of chunky mohair yarn in six bright colours: white, pink, green, turquoise, blue and purple. Several of these were oddments so the colours only appear once.
- The finished mandala measured approximately 51cm (20in) in diameter unstretched and stretched to 58.5cm (23in) once laid out wet on the ball.
- For the fibre, I used 300g of Corriedale carded wool sliver in bright pink (100g each for layers one and three) and a pink/purple mix (100g for layer two), alternating the layer colours to make the layout easier.
- For the opening, I butted up the edges as in the first variation project, leaving a 30cm (12in) long thin gap in the fibre. This ended up the same length after felting. To finish the project, I hand-sewed a 16in green zip to the inside of the felt and did quite a lot of trimming of the hairy mohair with scissors.
- I found that some of the mandala star points struggled to bond with the fibre, so after removing the felting ball and rubbing them I took some time to stitch any unbonded parts to the felt. I then carried on with the usual felting process, with the result that there was no sign of the stitches by the end as they had disappeared into the felt.
- The finished pouffe measures approximately 39.5cm (15.5in) in diameter, 96.5cm (38in) in circumference, and I used a 50cm (20in) diameter (100cm/40in circumference) round feather cushion pad. I've found that the larger cushion pads squish up very easily to create a deeper profile. In this case the finished depth was approximately 18cm (7in), which was perfect for a pouffe. Using the cushion pad to help shape the felt during fulling was key to achieving this.

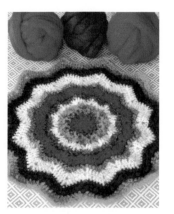

Crocheted mohair mandala and Corriedale carded wool fibre prior to felting.

Crocheted mandala laid out on the felting ball, covering the base down to the middle design line.

Pouffe during the felting stage, with neatened opening edge.

CHAPTER 4

ADDING EXTRA 3D STRUCTURE

Now that we have mastered the basic process of creating 3D forms using the felting ball, we can start to expand the structure to incorporate additional felted-in elements such as handles, flaps and metal hardware. Obviously we could create these elements separately and attach them by sewing or other methods like using metal rivets, glue or even creating holes to thread elements like cords through to make handles. But part of the uniqueness of felting is that we can create seamless bonds using wool fibre, which not only creates a neater, more unified and professional look but also brings great strength of bond to the elements we're attaching. So it seems wrong not to take advantage of that!

This chapter therefore introduces the concept of felting in extra elements and how best to approach it to achieve a successful and strong bond of those elements and create an integrated finished design. As in the previous chapter, I've included several projects which you could follow in full, plus some variation versions showing other ideas with a brief outline of how to make them, to help you get started.

HOW TO ADD EXTRA STRUCTURAL ELEMENTS

There are lots of ways you can approach a wet felting project which incorporates extra elements. For example, to create a felt bag with an integral handle using a flat resist you could create a large bag shape and cut an attached handle shape from it. This is trickier to achieve on the ball because we don't have lots of extra space to create a bigger area of felt from which we could cut out shapes. So I've found that the best approach is to create additional pieces separately, felting them as little as possible or just enough (to prefelt stage) so that they are able to keep their shape, but not so much that they are too felted to then attach to the main project. Generally I make those extra pieces first and add them during the fibre layout stage. It means that when you actually start the felting process they are already integrated with the rest of the fibre and will become a seamless part of the whole project by the end, without being an obvious add-on.

One of the most common structural elements you might want to add to a design is some kind of cord, whether to create a functional aspect like a handle, strap or closure, or a decorative item to create a spike or fringed effect. So let's start off by looking at an easy way to make a cord, through rolling a length of wool fibre. My example shows a thick cord, suitable for a bag strap, but the technique is the same for a thin cord. We're going to use a length of Merino combed tops fibre as the core for creating a smooth, rounded cord shape; for a thinner version, just peel a thinner strip from a length of tops fibre. I've found that using a length of Merino or other combed tops, which is in a long, even tube of fibre already, is one of the easiest and quickest ways of creating a smooth and durable cord. The other is by using carded wool sliver, which comes in a similar long length of fibre. The only downside is that using Merino might not match with the carded fibre or colour you're using for the rest of your project. But we can get around that by using Merino as the core, with another fibre covering it, and picking a Merino colour which closely matches the outside colour.

The sample version below shows exactly how to make a Merino cord and then cover it with a carded wool batt fibre if you are colour matching. If you want to make the cord out of just Merino, then omit Steps 5–7, but the rest of the felting process is the same. The key with cords is to start rolling with a light touch to avoid flattening them. Go gently to encourage the rounded shape and avoid flattening the tube until it feels firmer and is holding its shape, then you can apply more pressure. The sample also shows how to create a neat pointed end if you're going to use the cord separately or as a spike, as well as a prefelted version with an unfelted end for attaching to a main project on the ball.

The finished cord size was around 105cm (41.5cm) and weighed 30g. You'll note that the sample cord actually increased in length slightly. This is because most of the shrinkage happens to the thickness of the cord, and you get a bit of expansion to the length from the fibres stretching when first wet and actions like running your hand along it to shape it. In addition, I combined two very different wool fibre breeds, which will have affected the shrinkage. I've generally found that Merino-only cords shrink more in their length (the direction of the fibres) than ones made from batts and sliver (with their fibres going in all directions). So as always it's best to make a sample first to see how everything reacts together, particularly if you need an exact end size, but I'd generally always err on the side of going a bit bigger as you can always cut it down at prefelt stage.

Using Merino combed tops is not the only way of making a cord as you might also want to make them completely from the same carded wool fibre as your main project. So in the first project in this chapter, the Floral Basket Project, I demonstrate how to make cord handles used Bergschaf carded wool batt fibre. In the variation versions I show you how to use Corriedale carded wool sliver, a slightly different wool format again.

FELT CORD WITH FINISHED TAPERED ENDS

Materials
- 100cm (39.5in) (approximately 20g) length of Merino combed wool tops (I used pink)
- 100cm × 8cm (39.5in × 3in) (approximately 10g) strip of carded wool fibre (I used Maori as the pink was such a close match)

Equipment
- 110cm × 30cm (43in × 12in) piece of bubble wrap
- 50cm × 50cm (20in × 20in) piece of textured mat
- Tape measure
- Washing-up/dishwashing liquid
- Spray bottle containing washing-up liquid and warm water solution
- Several small/tea towels

Step by Step

Step 1: Collect your combed tops and carded fibre together and ensure a close colour match. Ensure your tops have wispy ends.

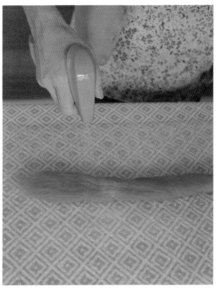

Step 2: Lay out your tops on the smooth side of the bubble wrap and untwist/straighten. Spray all over with soapy water to soak.

Step 3: Gently roll the tops away from you, lift, replace in front of you and roll it away again. Repeat rolling in one direction until it starts to hold its rounded shape.

Step 4: Alternate rolling in one direction with running your hand along it to encourage the rounded shape and tapered ends. Any cracks will disappear during felting.

Step 5: With the prefelt cord still squidgy but starting to hold the rounded shape as you roll, lay out the carded wool strip on the bubble wrap and place the cord on top.

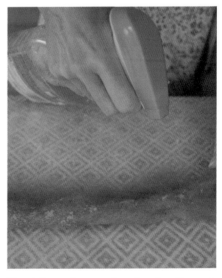

Step 6: Spray all over and gently roll up the cord in the carded fibre strip. Adjust the carded fibre at the ends to keep them wispy.

Step 7: Repeat Steps 3 and 4 to roll the covered cord very gently in one direction only and, once the rounded shape is holding, alternate with running your hands along it.

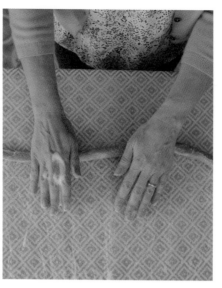

Step 8: Once the cord feels firmer and the surface is developing a smooth 'skin', start to gently roll back and forth.

Step 9: Roll more firmly back and forth as the cord starts to feel thicker. Note that the wispy ends naturally create a tapered point. Move the cord to the textured mat.

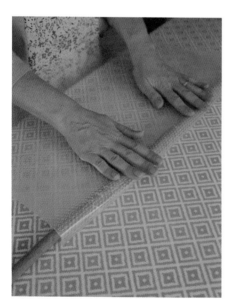

Step 10: Continue to roll the cord back and forth on the textured mat, applying more pressure. Then roll it inside the mat until it feels very firm and smooth-sided.

Step 11: Once the cord feels very firm and stays upright when you hold it up, rinse it in warm water to remove all soap and roll in a towel to remove excess water.

Step 12: Wipe the textured mat clean of soap and firmly roll the finished cord on it to reshape and smooth the surface. Leave to air dry.

PREFELT CORD WITH UNFINISHED ENDS

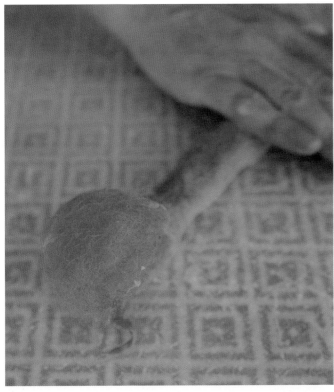

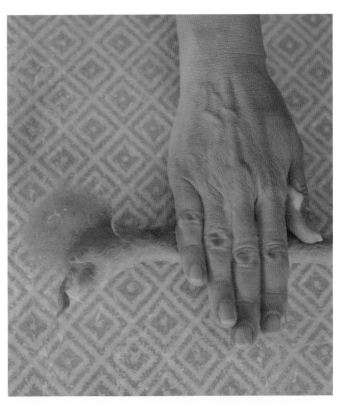

Follow Steps 1–7 above, leaving at least 5cm (2in) of fibre at each end as dry and fibrous as possible throughout the process.

Once the prefelt cord is still squidgy but just holding its rounded shape (between Steps 7–8), put aside without rinsing until ready to incorporate into your main project.

Preparation tip: to easily divide a length of combed wool tops fibre and create wispy ends, keep your hands far apart along the tops length and gently pull.

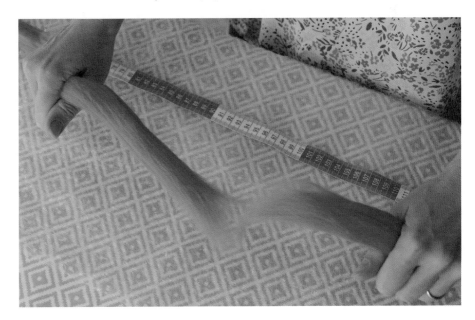

Useful Tips When Adding Structural Extras

Here are some extra tips I usually follow when adding additional elements to projects on the ball.

Make extra elements in advance

Because we ideally want to complete our layout on the ball in one session, due to issues like the fibre drying out, I've found it pays to create any extra elements first so that they are ready to attach when needed. That way you're not having to stop the layout on the ball to make them but can instead quickly attach/insert the extra pieces and move on. Some layouts can be quite time-consuming so you might want to make any extras the day before (just put them aside within bubble wrap layers) to avoid having to complete everything in one session.

Matching colours

To create a seamless colour match and non-obvious join I like to create my structural extras (flaps, handles and metal hardware) in the same colour as where they'll be most visible when attached, which is usually around the top outside edge of the finished felt (layer one). For projects where the inside of the finished felt is very obvious, such as a basket, I might also use the same colour inside the finished felt (layer three), or in a band around the top edge.

Inserting additional pieces

When inserting additional structural pieces during the layout, I like to insert them in the middle of layer two, to ensure that they are secured equally within the three fibre layers. Ensure that any edges or ends of items you are adding are wispy where they join the main fibre, for better integration.

Minimal felting

Err on the side of felting your structural extras less rather than more. For instance, when adding cord handles you'll ideally need completely unfelted ends, but you might find that when joining them to the main fibre you'll also want to add extra fibre further up the cord to strengthen and unify the join. It therefore helps if the cords are felted as little as possible so that they can still bond with any extra fibre. So save the full bonding, firming and shaping of them until later in the process once they are attached and you're fulling the rest of the project.

Working inside out

Remember that you're working inside out, so the right side of an item like a flap needs to be facing the ball when you add it.

Keeping extra elements in place

Avoid letting any structural elements which are only joined in one area (like a flap) hang down vertically into the propping-up bowl when you are completing the layout. The bowl slowly fills with water as you work, so you will find that the flap soaks up water, becomes sodden and then slides off when you next pick up the ball. So keep the flap rolled up slightly and propped against the side of the bowl to keep it in place.

Monitor your extras

Keep an eye on any structural extras as they are not constrained by being held in place around the ball like the main fibre and will therefore felt and shrink more quickly. So keep stretching and shaping them and, again, avoid felting them too much before you add them.

Dealing with a longer strap

Short cord handles will fit neatly on top of the ball, but if you're adding a long cord handle or strap and wondering what to do with the long central part, try coiling it around within the empty space at the top of the ball or even around the ball itself once the layout is complete. Use plastic to separate it from the rest of the layout to avoid them felting together.

Inside pockets

Several of the projects include an inside pocket, for which we include a separate rectangle resist template to create a hollow area in between layers. I usually insert this between layers two and three and include extra allocations of fibre above and below to give extra strength to each side of the pocket. I always keep the under pocket fibre colour the same as layer three, for colour mixing purposes, otherwise the template blocks the layer three colour in that area from migrating through to layers one and two. I generally leave the resist inside the pocket until rinsing. To neaten the pocket, put a finger into each side edge and gently stretch, before leaving to air dry.

Now that we've covered the basics of how to add structural extras to our main felt projects on the ball, let's move on to our first project, a basket with integral cord handles, so you can see how this works in practice.

FLORAL BASKET PROJECT

This project is a large open basket with two thick cord grab handles and a garden-inspired floral design, comprising variegated curly wool lock 'flowers' rising up all around the outside. The felt is made from two dark green shades of Bergschaf carded wool batt fibre to create a plain, seamless background to showcase the beautiful colours and textures of the curly locks.

To create the upright floral design we're working from the base, starting with the felting ball upside down. Curly wool locks will add a thick layer to the surface, which is good from a structural/sturdiness aspect but can also make them more difficult to felt in with the main wool fibre, especially when left in their very thick, tight curls. So it's a good idea to tease them apart to reduce the thickness and create some wispy space for the main wool fibre to penetrate through. Also avoid overlapping them too much, particularly at the base, as that's where all the ends of each upright lock are starting. So instead of starting them all at the base point, vary them so that some start a little further away. The locks will all have shifted and merged after shrinkage so even a little clear space left during layout will have filled in by the end.

As the locks become a bit unwieldy when dunked and placed on the ball, spray the ball first, then wisp out and place them, spraying the locks regularly to secure. That method gives you more control of their placement. You can also alternate heights and angles of how you place them. I used some locks with the finer tip end up, and some the other way up with the thicker end spread out, to vary the design. I slightly overlapped some of the wispy tips to give a more natural look.

As outlined in the previous section, we're prefelting the handles first before joining them to the main body of the basket, and keeping the ends as unfelted as possible. The prefelting helps them to maintain their rounded cord shape (because it's already been started off), whilst at the same time not felting them so much that it's hard to join them to the rest of the basket. The handles are very quick to make to prefelt stage, it doesn't take long at all to achieve a rounded shape with a smooth 'skin' whilst still very squidgy.

Part of the challenge is that we are making two identical handles, so it's important to start with the same weight and length of fibre for each. Prefelting them to the same stage and ensuring they are joined in the same way will ensure an even

Materials

- Approximately 160g of carded wool fibre in your chosen colours: 12g per handle (×2); and 45g per main layer (×3)
- I used Bergschaf carded wool batt fibre in the following combination:

Layout Element	Colour	Amount
Handles (×2)	Bright green	24g (12g each)
Layer 1	Bright green	15g
	Dark green	30g
Layer 2	Bright green	15g
	Dark green	30g
Layer 3	Bright green	45g

- Approximately 20g of long curly wool locks (I used a variety of Teeswater and Wensleydale variegated hand-dyed curly wool locks in greens, pinks and yellows)

Equipment

- Large purple felting ball, inflated to 91.5cm (36in) circumference
- Inflating pump
- 25cm (10in) internal diameter round bowl or similar to prop up the ball
- Large bowl of any size to hold the washing-up liquid and warm water solution
- 32cm (12.5in) minimum internal diameter round or square bowl to push rub the ball within
- Two pairs of XXL (137–152cm/54-60in hips) tights/pantyhose, 20 denier (see Chapter 1 for preparation)
- 100cm × 55cm (40in × 22in) piece of thin plastic
- 50cm × 50cm (20in × 20in) piece of textured mat
- Washing-up/dishwashing liquid
- Olive oil soap
- Spray bottle containing washing-up liquid and warm water solution
- Ball brause
- Several large towels
- Several small/tea towels
- Scales
- Tape measure
- Small scissors

pair of handles on the finished basket. The starting size we need for each handle, edge to edge (without overlapping the basket sides), is approximately 25cm (10in). So if we include a 5cm (2in) overlap each side, then our starting size should be approximately 35cm (14in). Cords made from carded wool batt and sliver tend not to shrink very much lengthways but, if in doubt, aim for a longer prefelt cord rather than shorter to ensure you have enough length for a good join.

Once you start felting, you'll find that the locks will felt to the fibre quite easily, so you can focus on integrating the handles. Throughout the whole process, and after every round of agitation, give the handle joins a spray and a rub, and shape the cords between your hands to maintain the cord shape. They will become firmer all the time and start maintaining

the rounded shape, so that by the end they will feel very firm and well integrated with the rest of the basket.

For the variation projects, I've included two similar floral basket versions with slight differences: one is a mini version of the main basket, with two cord handles; and the other is a mini version with one cord handle. Both use Corriedale carded wool sliver fibre, which shows another simple method of laying out fibre for felting cords.

The finished basket weighs approximately 180g and measures approximately 21.5cm wide/deep × 17cm high (24cm to the top of the handles) and 70cm in circumference (8.5in × 6.5in, 9.5in to the top of the handles, 27.5in in circumference). Each handle measures approximately 21cm (8in) from top edge to top edge.

Step by Step

Step 1: Assembling and preparing your materials

Collect your carded wool fibre and curly wool locks together to create a pleasing colour palette. Weigh 45g of wool fibre in your chosen colours for each of the three layers, and a 24g batt rectangle for the handles. Tear all fibre into palm-sized pieces, except the batt. Inflate the felting ball to 91.5cm (36in) in circumference.

Step 2: Preparing the handles

Take the 24g rectangle of batt and split the layers or divide into two equally sized 12g pieces, each measuring approximately 30cm × 20cm (12in × 8in). Place one piece in front of you oriented landscape-style on a textured mat. Tightly roll up the fibre away from you to create a long, tight tube and spray all over with soapy water.

Step 3: Rolling the first handle part 1

Gently roll the fibre tube away from you, lift, replace in front of you and gently roll it away from you again. Repeat rolling in one direction like this until the fibre tube feels a little firmer, is keeping its rounded shape and the surface is developing a smooth 'skin', then roll back and forth for a few minutes.

Step 4: Rolling the first handle part 2

The tube will have expanded slightly from 30cm (12in) to around 35cm (14in). Focus your hand pressure throughout on the central 20cm (8in) of the tube, leaving 5–7cm (2–3in) each end as unfelted as you can. Alternate rolling with smoothing your hand along the length of the tube to encourage the rounded shape.

Step 5: Rolling the second handle

Stop rolling when the tube is just keeping its rounded shape but is still slightly squidgy. Then repeat Steps 2–4 for the second fibre rectangle. Once both handles are at the same stage and look and feel very similar, stop rolling and put aside. Note that the fibre towards the handle ends should be quite expanded/unfelted.

Step 6: Adding curly wool locks

With the felting ball upside down on the propping-up bowl, spray the surface to help the curly wool locks stick. Take a long lock, tease out the fibres slightly and place on the ball, with the thicker end just off the centre base point and the thinner wispy end stopping approximately 2.5cm (1in) below the top edge line. Spray to secure in place.

Step 7: Completing the curly wool lock design

Repeat Step 6 to add more locks around the ball, varying the length and placement until happy with the overall design and spraying regularly to secure the locks in place. Try to ensure that the locks don't overlap too much, especially at the base, and aim for a single layer all over. Trim any locks as necessary to fit the design.

Step 8: Layer one fibre layout

Using the 45g fibre allocation for layer one (which I've divided into top third bright green and bottom two thirds dark green), take a piece of the dark green fibre, dunk it in soapy water, ensure it is spread out and completely soaked and place it directly on top of the base of the ball. Repeat to cover the base down to the middle design line.

Step 9: Finishing layers one and two fibre layout

Repeat Step 8 with the bright green fibre to cover the area of the ball from the middle design line to the top design line. Then go over the ball again, infilling thinner areas all over the ball in the appropriate colours until all the layer one fibre is used. Turn the ball the right way up and repeat Steps 8 and 9 with the layer two fibre allocation.

Step 10: Adding the first handle

Take the first handle, bend it in half and lay it on the top of the ball, with the bend at the plug and each half in line with one of the quarter segment lines. The handle should still be squidgy so flatten it against the ball to keep it in place. The unfelted ends should overlap the top of the main fibre. Spread the ends and spray to secure.

Step 11: Adding the second handle

From the layer three fibre allocation, add several pieces of fibre to cover each unfelted end of the handle. Repeat Steps 10 and 11 for the second handle. Check the handles from above to ensure the placements mirror each other and add any extra fibre to the ends and/or spray to ensure they feel securely in place.

Step 12: Layer three fibre layout

Add the 45g fibre allocation for layer three (I've used bright green only) to the ball using the same dunk and place method outlined in Steps 8 and 9 and patting regularly to check evenness. Add any extra fibre you feel necessary to thicken thin areas and around the handle joins. Spray the fibre all over and wrap in plastic.

Step 13: Preparing to rub the fibre

Stretch one pair of tights over the 32cm (12.5in) internal diameter rubbing bowl, place the ball inside with the plug facing downwards and gently pull up the edges of the tights as high as they will go. Repeat with the second pair of tights, this time placing the ball inside so that the area not covered by the first pair is covered.

Step 14: Rubbing the fibre

Place the ball inside the bowl, pour on soapy water to ensure the whole ball and tights are soaked, and gently push the ball around the bowl in all directions, ensuring that the ball makes contact with the sides of the bowl but not pushing so hard that the fibres are moved out of place. Repeat the pushing/rubbing action for 400 pushes.

Step 15: Neatening the edges

Peel each pair of tights away from the ball and back over the edges of the bowl, and place the ball on the propping-up bowl. Peel back the plastic to reveal the top edge of the fibre and handles. Neaten the top edge all around by fluffing up the edges, folding them outwards, spraying and gently rubbing. Replace the plastic and tights.

Step 16: Completing the rubbing

Repeat the push rub action for 400 pushes twice more, pushing more firmly each time. Remove the ball from the tights/plastic after each round, then spray and rub the top edge and handle joins to ensure integration with the main fibre, soaking and rubbing both inside and out (you will be able to get your hand just inside to do this).

Step 17: Bouncing the ball

Place the ball in the tights and bounce it on your work surface 500 times. The easiest method is to hold the tights above the ball whilst bouncing. After 500 bounces, remove the tights/plastic to check/rub the edges and handle joins as before. Repeat this process at least twice more, alternating ball placement in the tights each time.

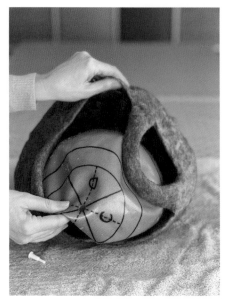

Step 18: Removing the ball

The fibre around the ball should now feel much firmer, tighter and thicker. If not, replace the tights and complete a further round of 500 bounces or more until the fibre is feeling more solid and fully integrated with itself. Remove the tights and plastic, deflate the ball and remove it from the prefelt basket shape.

Step 19: Rubbing the wool locks

Next give the inside of the basket a good soapy shower. Check whether the curly wool locks have felted to the inside by gently running your fingers across them. If they are still moving or not fully adhered, with a very wet and soapy hand do some focused rubbing along the direction of the locks until they stay firmly in place.

Step 20: Rubbing the handles

Now that the ball has been removed, you can also focus on rubbing and shaping the flattened prefelted handles to return them to their rounded cord shape. With very wet, soapy hands rub and roll each handle between your palms to encourage the rounded shape until they feel very firm. Also rub firmly around the handle joins.

Step 21: Throwing the basket

Loosely pick up the basket and throw it on the work surface 25 times, spinning the basket around on its sides as you throw and maintaining the rounded basket shape at all times. After 25 throws, reshape it and rub the inside, top edge and handles. Throw another 25 if still delicate, or 50 if feeling firmer, and repeat rubbing/shaping.

Step 22: Completing the throwing

Repeat Step 21 to complete 200 throws in total. The felt should be starting to shrink, feel thicker and be developing a crinkled texture. Turn the basket the right side out, reshape and then repeat a further two rounds of 100 throws in the same way as Step 21, along with throwing the basket with its base on the table to flatten and shape it.

Step 23: Shaping the basket

Your felt basket should now feel thick and sturdy and be keeping its shape and structure. If not, continue to alternate between throwing it on its side, throwing it on its base, shaping/stretching the inside and sides with your hands and rubbing the handles until you are satisfied with the overall basket shape and structure.

Step 24: Finishing the basket

Rinse the basket under warm running water, or soak in bowls of warm water, squeezing gently until the water runs clear. Alternate between warm and cold water rinses if the felt still needs firming. Remove excess water by rolling the basket up in a dry towel, then reshape and leave to air dry on a towel.

MINI FLORAL BASKET WITH DOUBLE CORD HANDLES

For the first variation I made a mini basket with two cord handles, which nests neatly into the larger green version so would be perfect for making sets. I used pretty much the same combination of curly wool locks (15g) as embellishment, but added some wispy blend fibres on top (5g) and changed the wool fibre to variegated Corriedale carded sliver. Here are the main details on how I made this version:

- Small green felting ball, inflated to 76cm (30in) in circumference.
- For the main body of the basket, 100g of Corriedale carded wool sliver, divided into: layers one and two, turquoise and green (33g per layer); layer three turquoise (34g).
- For each handle, 10g of turquoise sliver in a 25cm (10in) length. As the sliver was quite thin, the 25cm consisted of four separate lengths. I kept 2.5cm (1in) dry at each end, focusing on the central 20cm (8in) to create the prefelted part.

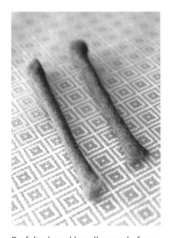

Prefelted cord handles made from Corriedale carded wool sliver fibre.

Embellishment layout of curly wool locks and carded blend fibres.

Completed wool fibre layout, including handles, prior to felting.

Size comparison of main and mini project baskets.

MINI FLORAL BASKET WITH SINGLE CORD HANDLE

For the second basket variation project I created another mini version, in eggshell pink and white Corriedale carded wool sliver fibre with a single cord handle instead of two. The wool fibre and measurements are all the same as for the mini double cord handles version, except that I created just one handle using 12g of eggshell pink fibre in a 35cm (13.75in) length (again, consisting of four separate, thinner lengths) and kept 5cm (2in) dry at each end. I used a similar curly wool locks combination as before but omitted the blend fibres on top. Aside from only having a single handle, it's interesting to compare how different the curly locks and basket overall look with a very pale background colour compared to the main dark green version.

Dry fibre layout of handle, made from Corriedale carded wool sliver fibre.

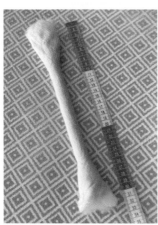

Prefelted cord handle ready to attach.

Embellishment layout of curly wool locks on the ball.

Completed wool fibre layout, including handle, prior to felting.

DARTMOOR BASKET BAG PROJECT

This is a large bag project but with the additional effect of a basket and with two different carrying options: flat grab bag handles as well as a longer detachable cross-body or shoulder strap. The narrow base and raised-up handles give a large surface area front and back to display a design. Like the preceding Floral Basket Project, it has a floral theme and uses curly wool locks, but in more of a watercolour landscape design created by layering up a variety of textured embellishment materials, including chunky mohair bouclé yarns. I live quite close to Dartmoor National Park in Devon and I've tried to reflect its rich colours of heather and moors. So I've included a tweed blend tops fibre, which seemed appropriate for the

WHAT YOU WILL NEED

Materials

- Approximately 210g of carded wool fibre in your chosen colours: 55g each for layers one and two (including handles); 60g for layer three (including handles); 35g above and below the pocket; and 4g for the D-ring tabs (×2)
- I used Corriedale carded wool sliver fibre in the following combination:

Layout Element	Colour	Amount
D-ring tabs (×2)	Pink	4g (2g each)
Layer 1	Pink	15g
	Mid green	15g
	Dark green	15g
Layer 1 handles (×2)	Pink	10g (5g each)
Layer 2	Pink	15g
	Mid green	15g
	Dark green	15g
Layer 2 handles (×2)	Pink	10g (5g each)
Under pocket	Lilac	10g
Over pocket	Lilac	25g
Layer 3	Lilac	50g
Layer 3 handles (×2)	Lilac	10g (5g each)

- Approximately 10g of curly wool locks (I used a variety of Teeswater and Wensleydale variegated hand-dyed curly wool locks in greens, pinks and purples)
- Approximately 3–5m (10–16ft) each of at least three wool yarns (I used a mix of chunky mohair bouclé and straight mohair yarns in green and pink shades)
- Approximately 30g of a blended tops lustre fibre (I used tweed-effect tops in pink and green)
- 2 × 25mm (1in) metal D-rings (I used antique brass)
- 2.5cm (1in) leather-backed sew-on magnetic clasp (I used brown to match the bag strap colour)
- Sewing thread to match the clasp (I used brown)
- Long cross-body bag strap with metal lobster clasp (or similar) ends. (I used a 120cm × 18mm/47in × 0.75in brown leather strap)

Equipment

For the wet felting
- Large purple felting ball, inflated to 91.5cm (36in) circumference
- Inflating pump
- 24cm high × 18cm wide (9.5in × 7in), 1–2mm thin foam or plastic pocket resist template (*see* Chapter 8, Templates and Tables)
- 25cm (10in) internal diameter round bowl or similar to prop up the ball
- Large bowl of any size to hold the washing-up liquid and warm water solution
- 32cm (12.5in) minimum internal diameter round or square bowl to push rub the ball within
- Two pairs of XXL (137–152cm/54–60in hips) tights/pantyhose, 20 denier (*see* Chapter 1 for preparation)
- 100cm × 55cm (40in × 22in) piece of thin plastic
- 25cm × 25cm (10in × 10in) piece of bubble wrap
- Washing-up/dishwashing liquid
- Olive oil soap
- Spray bottle (containing washing-up liquid and warm water solution)
- Ball brause
- Several large towels
- Several small/tea towels
- Scales
- Tape measure
- Ruler
- Permanent marker pen
- Large and small scissors

For sewing the clasp
- Tape measure
- Pins
- Sewing needle
- Scissors

countryside landscape feel, but you could substitute this for any speciality tops or carded blends, including art batts. For the main fibre I've used Corriedale carded wool sliver in pink, lilac and green shades, and similar colours for the mohair yarn and curly wool locks. I've used darker colours at the bottom moving up to lighter shades, to give a more landscape-like feel.

Structurally, the handles are flat and more of an extension of the main fibre, in contrast to the added cord handles in the Floral Basket Project. Our structural extras this time are felted-in D-rings each side for attaching a longer strap. The bag also features a large inside pocket, and a magnetic clasp closure on the inside. In Chapter 7 I show you a way to hand-sew a clasp like this one so that it's invisible from the outside.

During the layout stage, if there is a definite front and back to your design, you might want to note the corresponding letters from the top of the ball so that you know which side to add your pocket. I always add them to the back of a bag just in case there is any distortion to the outside design caused by the pocket inside. Of course you don't have to include a pocket at all if you prefer, or you could have one each side! I created a large pocket for this bag but you could make it smaller by reducing the template size slightly.

The finished bag weighs approximately 275g (with D-rings and clasp) and measures approximately 30cm wide × 27cm high × 12cm deep (12in × 10.5in × 4.75in). Each handle width measures approximately 2.5cm (1in).

Step by Step

Step 1: Assembling and preparing your materials

Collect your carded wool fibre and embellishments together to create a pleasing colour palette. Weigh out all fibre allocations, tear all carded wool (not the tops blend) into palm-sized pieces and keep separate. Inflate the felting ball to 91.5cm (36in) in circumference and place it upside down on the propping-up bowl.

Step 2: Prepare the pocket resist template

Take the 24cm high × 18cm wide (9.5in × 7in) rectangular 1–2mm thin foam pocket resist template and mark a horizontal line going across the template 6cm (2.5in) down from the top/18cm (7in) up from the bottom. This line marks where the fibre layout goes up to. Then mark a central vertical dotted line 9cm (3.5in) from either side.

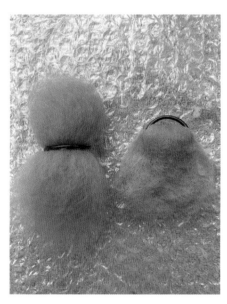

Step 3: Preparing the D-ring tabs

Working on bubble wrap, take a D-ring and 2g tab fibre allocation and tear the fibre to create an 8cm × 4cm (3in × 1.5in) rectangle. Roll the fibre lengthways to create a tube and place it through the D-ring. Fold each half of fibre down around the straight bar of the ring. Dunk in soapy water. Repeat for the second tab and put both aside.

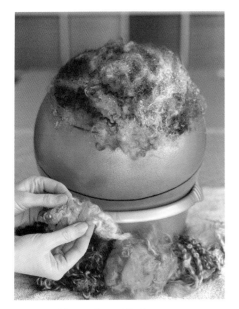

Step 4: Adding curly wool locks

Spray the surface of the ball to help the curly wool locks stick. Take a lock, tease out the fibres, place on the ball and spray to secure. Repeat to build up a single layer of locks laid horizontally around the ball, covering the whole base and down to midway between the base edge and middle design lines. Spray regularly to secure.

Step 5: Adding textured yarns

Take the first mohair bouclé yarn, unwind at least 1m (40in) and dunk it in the soapy water, without cutting it. Starting with the loose end, wrap the soapy yarn around the ball in a wavy organic line at least three times, then cut off. Repeat for the other textured yarns, covering the area from where the locks end to the middle design line.

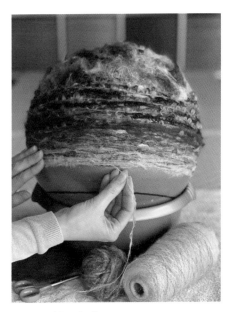

Step 6: Adding further yarns

Repeat Step 5 to add straighter and finer mohair yarns, continuing from where the previous yarns ended and covering up to midway between the middle and top design lines. Overlap yarns slightly to build up a pleasing design but still keep them slightly wavy. Add any further yarns or locks now to complete the design.

Step 7: Adding blend fibres

Take a 100cm (39.5in), 7g length of green tweed tops and spread it out to a width of 5cm. Place it in a band around the ball from the end of the curly locks to the middle design line and press. Repeat with a 100cm (39.5in), 13g length of pink tweed tops spread out to a width of 10cm and placed from the middle to the top design line.

Step 8: Layer one fibre layout

Using the 45g main fibre allocation for layer one (which I've divided into thirds colourwise), take a piece of the dark green fibre, dunk it in soapy water, ensure it is spread out and completely soaked and place it directly on top of the base of the ball. Repeat to cover the base down to the start of the green tweed tops band.

Step 9: Finishing layer one fibre layout

Repeat Step 8 with the mid green fibre to cover the area of the ball from the dark green fibre up to the middle design line. Then repeat with the pink fibre from the middle to the top design line. Then go over the ball again, infilling thinner areas all over the ball in the appropriate colours until all the layer one fibre is all used.

Step 10: Laying out the first handle

Turn the ball plug side up and peel back the top edge of pink fibre slightly to reveal the pink tweed tops. Divide the remaining 10g of pink tweed tops into two and use wisps of the first 5g to set out the first handle shape at the top of the ball. Note that the handle width is 4cm (1.5in) and the hole 12cm × 4cm (4.75in × 1.5in). Spray to hold.

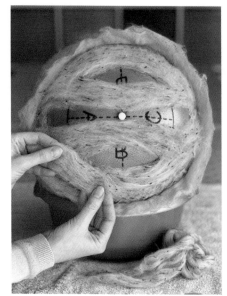

Step 11: Laying out the second handle

Repeat Step 10 to set out the shape of the second handle using the remaining 5g allocation of pink tweed tops, as shown. Note that you are leaving a narrow gap between the two handles where the plug sits. Also that the gap widens to follow the top curve of the handles and extends down to the top design line.

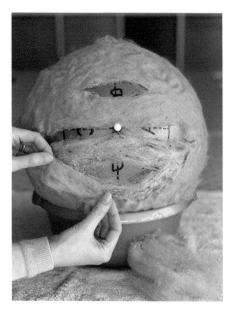

Step 12: Laying out further handle fibre

Divide the 10g fibre allocation for the layer one handles into two and repeat steps 10 and 11 to cover the pink tweed tops handle shapes with the pink carded wool fibre using the dunk and place method. The layer one layout is now complete. Pat the ball and, if any area feels slightly thinner at this stage, add extra pink fibre now.

Step 13: Adding the side tabs

Take two pieces of the pink 15g layer two fibre allocation and add them to the small visible area of the bag's top edge at one side in between the handles (up to the top design line). Re-soak one of the tabs and add it on top of the fibre, with the hidden straight edge of the D-ring in line with the top design line. Repeat for the second tab.

Step 14: Layer two fibre layout

Add the rest of the 55g fibre allocation for layer two, which includes the 10g allocation for the handles, starting with covering the top of the tab fibre up to the top design line, leaving just the curved bar of the D-rings poking out from the top. Follow the same colour layout as for layer one.

Step 15: Adding the under pocket fibre

Take the 10g lilac under pocket allocation and add it to one side of the bag in an approximate 22cm wide × 28cm long (8.5in × 11in) rectangle starting immediately below the handle hole and oriented centrally to the handle. The rectangle does not need to be precise, just larger than the resist template.

Step 16: Adding the pocket resist template

Wet the pocket resist template and place it on top of the under pocket fibre, with the top of the template starting 2.5cm (1in) below the handle hole. The central dotted line should match up with the dotted top placement line on the ball and be central to the handle. Start to add pocket fibre on top, overlapping the side edges of the template.

Step 17: Adding the pocket fibre

Add the full 25g lilac pocket fibre allocation on top of the resist template. Add the fibre using the usual dunk and place method, going up to the marked line on the template and overlapping the three edges of the template by 2–3cm (1in) to join the under pocket fibre. Lay out the fibre as evenly as possible all over the template.

Step 18: Layer three fibre layout

Add the full 60g lilac fibre allocation for layer three, which includes the 10g handle allocation. Cover all the existing fibre layout on the ball, including over the tabs, the handles, the pocket (up to the marked line on the template) and the area under the loose top of the template (down to the marked line on the template's reverse).

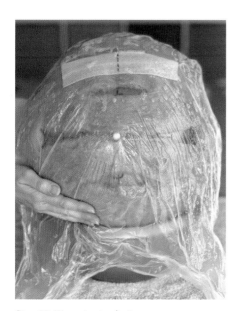

Step 19: Wrapping in plastic

Pat the fibre to check evenness and add any extra fibre you feel necessary to thicken thin areas. Check that there is still a small gap at the plug between the two handles. Generously spray the fibre all over and wrap in plastic.

Step 20: Preparing to rub the fibre

Stretch one pair of tights over the 32cm (12.5in) rubbing bowl, place the ball inside with the plug facing downwards and gently pull up the edges of the tights as high as they will go. Repeat with the second pair of tights, this time placing the ball inside so that the area not covered by the first pair is covered.

Step 21: Rubbing the fibre

Place the ball inside the bowl, pour on soapy water to ensure the whole ball and tights are soaked, and gently push the ball around the bowl in all directions, ensuring that the ball makes contact with the sides of the bowl but not pushing so hard that the fibres are moved out of place. Repeat the pushing/rubbing action for 400 pushes.

Step 22: Neatening the edges

Remove the tights and peel back the plastic. Neaten the edges all around by fluffing them up, spraying, folding them outwards and gently rubbing. Check and adjust the handles and handle holes to look and measure the same: handles approximately 4cm wide (1.5in) and the holes approximately 11cm × 3cm (4.25in × 1.25in).

Step 23: Neatening the pocket

Neaten the pocket edge in the same way as Step 22 by fluffing up the fibre, spraying, folding it outwards and gently rubbing. Replace the plastic and tights.

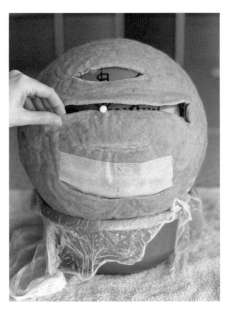

Step 24: Completing the rubbing

Repeat the push rub action for 400 pushes twice more, making 1,200 in total, pushing more firmly each time. Remove the ball from the tights/ plastic after each round and reshape the handles, which will have moved around and pushed up together. Also spray and rub all the folded edges to ensure good fibre bonds and neat shapes.

Step 25: Bouncing the ball

Place the ball in the tights and bounce it on your work surface 500 times. The easiest method is to hold the tights above the ball whilst bouncing. After 500 bounces, remove the tights/plastic to check/rub the edges and reshape the handles. Repeat this process three more times, alternating ball placement in the tights each time.

Step 26: Removing the ball

The fibre around the ball should now feel much firmer, tighter and thicker. If not, replace the tights and complete a further round of 500 bounces or more until the fibre is feeling more solid and fully integrated with itself. Remove the tights and plastic, deflate the ball and remove it from the prefelt bag shape.

Step 27: Rubbing the embellishments

Give the inside of the bag a warm soapy shower. Check whether the curly wool locks and yarns have felted to the inside by gently running your fingers across them. If they are still moving or not fully adhered, with a very wet and soapy hand do some focused rubbing along the direction they are laid until they stay firmly in place.

Step 28: Rubbing and throwing the bag

Dunk the bag in warm soapy water. With soapy hands, rub around the handles, top edge and tabs to start to shape and firm them. Then, with one hand inside the bag, loosely pick it up and throw it on the work surface 50 times, spinning the bag around on its sides as you throw. Then rub the inside embellishments again if still loose.

Step 29: Continuing to rub and throw the bag

Continue to throw the bag in groups of 50, alternating between rubbing the inside embellishments and rubbing/shaping the handles, top edge and tabs each time. Also rub the pocket to flatten it overall and neaten the pocket edge. Once the bag is starting to feel firmer after approximately 200–250 throws, turn it right side out.

Step 30: Completing the throwing

With your hands inside, stretch and reshape the bag to set the tabs at the sides and create a narrow depth. Continue to throw the bag on the work surface in groups of 50, up to 200, this time keeping its flatter shape and flipping it onto alternate sides every ten throws. Reshape after every 50, including flattening the pocket inside.

Step 31: Shaping the bag

Your bag should now feel thick and sturdy and be keeping its shape and structure. If not, continue to alternate between shaping/stretching the inside and sides, rubbing and shaping the handles, throwing it on alternate sides, flattening the inside pocket and flattening the base, until you are satisfied with the overall shape and structure.

Step 32: Rinsing the bag

Remove the pocket resist. Rinse the bag under warm running water, or soak in bowls of warm water, squeezing gently until the water runs clear. Alternate between hot and cold water rinses if the felt still needs firming. Remove excess water by rolling the bag up in a dry towel, then reshape and leave to air dry on a towel.

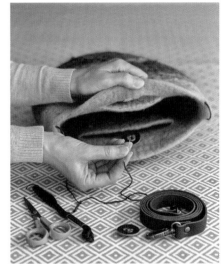

Step 33: Finishing the bag

To attach a leather-backed sew-on magnetic clasp fastener, positioned centrally under the handles, follow the Invisible Clasp Stitching Method outlined in Chapter 7. For a different type of sew-on magnetic clasp, *see* the Mandala Crochet Cushion Project in Chapter 3. Then clip on a long bag strap to the D-rings to finish.

HANGING BASKET SET

This variation project uses a similar flat handle method to the main project to create a set of two single-handle hanging baskets in different sizes. I used a hand-dyed braid of Corriedale combed wool tops in blues and oranges for the outer colours of both baskets, with Corriedale carded wool sliver for the insides. Despite being in tops form, the braid fibre kept its structure well enough to dunk and use on the ball. Here are the main points to note about how I made these:

- The larger basket used the green felting ball inflated to 76cm (30in) in circumference and approximately 100g of fibre. I used hand-dyed Corriedale for layers one and two (33g per layer, including handle) and solid green Corriedale for layer three (33g).
- The smaller basket used the green felting ball inflated to 66cm (26in) in circumference and approximately 70g of fibre. I used hand-dyed Corriedale for layers one and two (23g per layer, including handle) and solid orange Corriedale for layer three (23g).
- For the handle layouts, I used one main top placement segment of the ball as the overall width guide at the base of each handle, which looped around the top plug. The handle width was approximately 4.5cm (1.75in) for the larger basket and 4cm (1.5in) for the smaller one, which became 2.5cm (1in) and 2cm (0.75in) respectively after felting.
- Opposite the handles I lowered the top edge gradually to make the top more accessible when the baskets are hanging up.

- Interestingly, despite using the same sheep breed of fibre (Corriedale) for both baskets, the difference in types of fibre (finer hand-dyed combed tops at 26.5 microns versus coarser commercially dyed carded sliver at 29–30 microns) for the layers has made quite a difference to the inside versus outside texture of the finished baskets. This indicates that the fibres haven't felted at the same rate, with the hand-dyed, combed fibre appearing to have felted faster, causing the bumpier texture of the slower-felting inside fibre.

Hand-dyed braid of Corriedale combed wool tops used for the outer basket layers.

Larger basket: completed layer two (hand-dyed Corriedale) fibre layout.

Larger basket: completed layer three (green Corriedale) fibre layout after neatening the edges during the rubbing stage.

Smaller basket: completed layer three (orange Corriedale) fibre layout after neatening the edges during the rubbing stage.

Green felting ball used as a finishing forma to shape the larger basket during drying.

Nesting baskets.

BACKPACK PROJECT

This design is more of a challenge because of the many processes involved, but I hope you'll find it worth it to create this roomy backpack which converts in a split second to a shoulder or cross-body bag! Its other features are: a flap and clasp closure; inside and outside pockets; and a felted strap. However, you can adapt these features as much as you like, so you could omit the pockets, change the clasp or buy a length of webbing or leather strap rather than make your own.

There are several structural extras which we're adding to the basic round design, namely a large flap closure and felted-in metal rings, as well as the pockets. The most critical aspect to make the design work is the rings, because they enable you to easily attach a strap and use the bag as both a backpack and, by pulling the strap upwards through the D-rings, a shoulder bag. We therefore need to add extra markings to the ball before we start, to mark up their position. (NB: For the purposes of this project, Area A will signify the front of the backpack, C the back of the backpack, and B and D the sides.) If you're adding a front pocket, it's also important to get that positioning correct so that you're able to fold the flap over and attach the closure clasp to it. Chapter 7 shows you in detail how to install a clasp on a flap.

Fibre-wise, I've used Finnwool carded wool batt fibre in red and navy blue on the outside, with orange inside. Surface design-wise, you can use any embellishments you prefer. I've used a mixture of my favourite embellishment materials to build up an abstract landscape-like design: chunky wool yarns in a spiral on the base, leading up to a mix of mohair and bouclé yarns in the middle area and silk hankies around the top and on the flap. Just bear in mind that, for a seamless overall design, you'll want to carry over some of the embellishment materials to your extra elements. So you'll see I've added silk fibres to the top of the outside front pocket and to the flap as well as the ball, so that the embellishments will continue onto those extra pieces.

As this is a more complex project with lots of separate processes, I'd recommend dividing it up into stages which could each be completed on separate days, although it may be best to complete all the embellishment and wool fibre layout in one session. As the layout takes a while, you will need to keep spraying the fibre to ensure it doesn't dry out, and use plastic to hold it in place. The only thing to watch out for is keeping the metal rings within wet felt for too long as I've found they start to go rusty. So avoid leaving the extra structural items for longer than a day before adding them to the layout.

The finished backpack weighs approximately 330g with rings, clasp and strap, and measures approximately 30.5cm wide × 28cm high × 10cm deep (12in × 11in × 4in).

WHAT YOU WILL NEED

Materials

Carded wool fibre: Finnwool fibre prior to main preparation (not including the strap).

Embellishment materials: silk hankies and mix of chunky wool and mohair yarns.

Metal hardware: antique brass-coloured rings and clasp.

- Approximately 230g of carded wool batt fibre in your chosen colours: 50g each for the three layers; 40g for pockets and tabs; 20g for the flap; and 20g for the strap
- I used Finnwool carded wool batt fibre in the following three-colour combination:

Layout Element	Colour	Amount
Outside front pocket	Red	5g
	Navy	10g
Flap	Red	20g
		(in a 27cm × 25cm/ 10.5in × 10in batt piece)
Top D-ring tabs (×2)	Red	2g (1g each)
Back ring tabs (×2)	Navy	2g (1g each)
Layer 1	Red	25g
	Navy	25g
Layer 2	Red	25g
	Navy	25g
Under inside back pocket	Orange	5g
Over inside back pocket	Red	16g
Layer 3	Orange	50g
Strap	Red	20g
		(in a 150cm × 12cm/ 59in × 4.5in batt strip)

- Approximately 5g of silk hankies (I used variegated red colours)
- Approximately 3–5m (10–16ft) each of at least three wool yarns (I used nine in total, comprising a mix of mohair bouclé, straight mohair and chunky thick and thin wool yarns in red, navy, orange and yellow shades)
- 2 × 25mm (1in) width metal D-rings
- 2 × 25mm (1in) width metal rectangle rings (minimum 2cm/0.75in high)
- 2 × 25mm (1in) width metal rectangle sliding adjuster rings (minimum 2cm/0.75in high)
- 37cm × 21cm (approximately 1in) metal turn-lock clasp

Equipment

- Large purple felting ball, inflated to 91.5cm (36in) circumference
- Inflating pump
- 18cm high × 16cm wide (7in × 6.25in), 1–2mm thin foam or plastic outside front pocket resist template (*see* Chapter 8, Templates and Tables)
- 35cm high × 14cm wide (9.5in × 7in), 1–2mm thin foam or plastic inside back pocket resist template (*see* Chapter 8, Templates and Tables)
- 25cm (10in) internal diameter round bowl or similar to prop up the ball
- Large bowl of any size to hold the washing-up liquid and warm water solution
- 32cm (12.5in) minimum internal diameter round or square bowl to push rub the ball within
- Two pairs of XXL (137–152cm/54–60in hips) tights/pantyhose, 20 denier (*see* Chapter 1 for preparation)
- 100cm × 55cm (40in × 22in) piece of thin plastic
- Bubble wrap: 40cm × 25cm (16in × 10in) piece (outside front pocket); 55cm × 30cm (22in × 12in) piece (flap): 25cm × 25cm (10in × 10in) piece (back tabs)
- Washing-up/dishwashing liquid
- Olive oil soap
- Spray bottle containing washing-up liquid and warm water solution
- Ball brause
- Several large towels
- Several small/tea towels
- Scales
- Tape measure
- Ruler
- Permanent marker pen
- Small scissors
- Pegs

Step by Step

Step 1: Assembling and preparing your materials

Collect your carded wool fibre and embellishments together to create a pleasing colour palette. Weigh out all fibre allocations, tear all carded wool into palm-sized pieces (except the flap and strap fibre allocations, which should be kept in batt rectangles and strips respectively – *see* Materials above) and keep separate.

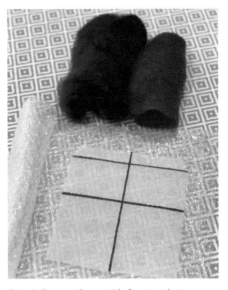

Step 2: Prepare the outside front pocket resist template

Take the 18cm high × 16cm wide (7in × 6.25in) rectangular 1–2mm thin foam outside front pocket resist template and mark the horizontal and vertical lines as shown in Chapter 8, Templates and Tables. Note that the horizontal line 2cm (0.75in) down marks the top edge flap fold line, and the line 8cm (3.25in) down marks the fibre colour change line.

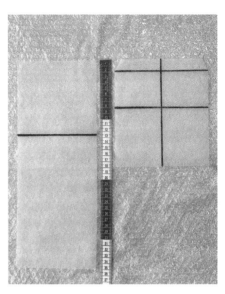

Step 3: Prepare the inside back pocket resist template

Take the 35cm high × 14cm wide (14in × 5.5in) rectangular 1–2mm thin foam inside back pocket resist template and mark a horizontal line going across the template 13cm (5in) down from the top edge as shown in Chapter 8, Templates and Tables. This line marks where the fibre layout goes up to.

Step 4: Marking the centre front line of the ball

Inflate the felting ball to 91.5cm (36in) in circumference. To mark the centre front line of the ball, lay the tape measure from the centre of the plug along the existing dotted line in the A segment right down to the base centre point of the ball. Mark on the middle design line and the base edge line where the tape measure intersects them.

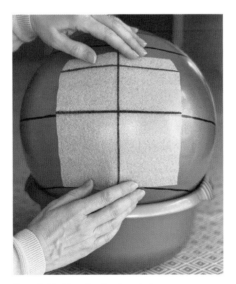

Step 5: Marking the front pocket placement points 1

To mark the outside front pocket placement points, place the outside front pocket template on the ball, with the bottom centre edge of the template meeting the base edge line of the ball, and the central vertical line of the template matching the two centre front line marks on the middle design line and the base edge line of the ball.

Step 6: Marking the front pocket placement points 2

Ensure the template flap is folded down so that the overall shape is now a 16cm × 16cm (6.25in × 6.25in) square. Mark each corner of the square template on the ball. Note that the bottom corner markings will be just above the base edge line (not on it), as we are working on a sphere.

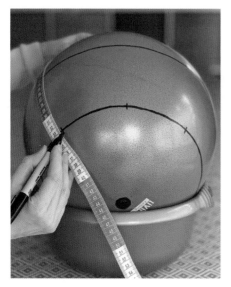

Step 7: Marking the back bottom tabs placement

Repeat Step 4 down from the C segment dotted line to mark the centre back line of the ball on the base edge line. To mark the bottom tabs placement, lay the tape measure from the plug along each of the existing two solid lines of the C segment down to the base centre point and mark where they intersect the base edge line.

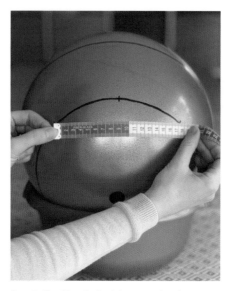

Step 8: Checking the back bottom tabs placement

To check the back bottom tabs placement, note that the two marks will be approximately 17cm (6.75in) apart (using a straight line). Each tab placement mark will also (again, using a straight line) measure approximately 9cm (3.5in) to the centre back line which is marked in between them on the base edge line.

Step 9: Preparing the outside front pocket 1

Place the pocket template on one half of the 40cm × 25cm (16in × 10in) piece of bubble wrap and lay the 15g fibre allocation on top, with the 5g red in the top third and the 10g navy in the bottom two thirds, creating an even layer. Overlap the top edge of the template slightly but overlap the other three edges by at least 2.5cm (1in).

Step 10: Preparing the outside front pocket 2

Spray to soak, cover with the other bubble wrap half and flatten. Turn the package over to the reverse, peel back the bubble wrap and spray the fibre under the template. Fold the template flap and top edge of fibre under to create a thick, neat top edge at the fold. Wisp out the fibre where it extends at the top sides.

Step 11: Decorating the outside front pocket

Turn the package to the front. Once on the ball, the top 2cm (1in) of the pocket front will remain covered by the template flap (to maintain the pocket opening) so will not pick up any embellishment materials. In order to keep the design consistent in this area, add some silk fibres to the top of the pocket under the flap. Put aside.

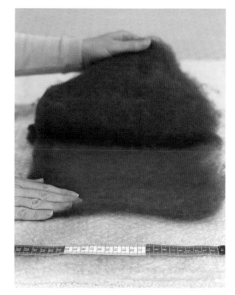

Step 12: Preparing the flap 1

Divide the 27cm × 25cm (10.5in × 9.5in) rectangle of red batt fibre in half thickness-wise by peeling into two layers each weighing 10g. Keep the thickness of each piece even and the edges wispy. Place the first piece on one half of the 55cm × 30cm (22in × 12in) piece of bubble wrap, oriented portrait-style in front of you.

Step 13: Preparing the flap 2

Spray to soak, cover with the other bubble wrap half and flatten. Turn the package over, peel back the bubble wrap and spray as necessary. Fold over the edges on three sides (two long and one short side) by approximately 2–3cm (1in) to create a curved rectangle 25cm high × 22cm wide (9.5in × 8.5in). Keep the near short edge four wispy.

Step 14: Preparing the flap 3

Place the two metal D-rings on top of the flap, each with the curve pointing upwards and the straight bar 17cm (6.5in) from the tip of the flap, 2.5cm (1in) from each side edge and 10cm (4in) apart. Cut two 2.5cm (1in) slits in the flap to match the position of the 2.5cm (1in) straight bar of each metal D-ring.

Step 15: Preparing the flap 4

Take a 1g tab allocation of red fibre and shape it into a 6cm × 3cm (2.25in × 1in) rectangle. Place it through one of the metal D-rings. Then push the curved part of the D-ring into the slit in the flap through to the other side. This leaves the tab fibre spread out on top of the flap with the straight bar visible. Repeat for the second tab.

Step 16: Preparing the flap 5

Spray the tab fibre to flatten. Lay the second fibre rectangle on top, overlapping all edges, and spray. Cover with bubble wrap and flatten, then turn over the package to the front of the flap. Fold excess fibre from the second layer over the curved edges. Add extra wisps through each protruding ring to cover the slits and spray to secure.

Step 17: Decorating the flap

Add silk or other fibres on top of the front of the flap (which will join up with the fibres on the ball) and spray to secure. Note that the D-rings should be folded down flat, with the curves facing towards the curved tip of the flap. Cover with bubble wrap and put aside.

Step 18: Preparing the back bottom tabs 1

Working on one half of the 25cm × 25cm (10in × 10in) piece of bubble wrap, take a 1g navy back tab fibre allocation and shape it into a 6cm × 3cm (2.25in × 1in) rectangle. Push it through a metal rectangle ring so that the ring sits in the centre of it. Repeat with the second tab fibre allocation and rectangle ring and put one aside.

Step 19: Preparing the back bottom tabs 2

From the main layer one 25g navy allocation, lay three to five pieces of fibre on top of one another and spray to secure and flatten. Cut a 2.5cm (1in) slit in the centre of the fibre. Take the tab and push one of the long bars of the ring through the slit, leaving the tab fibre securing the other long bar on the reverse. Repeat for the second tab.

Step 20: Preparing the back bottom tabs 3

Ensure the tab fibre on the reverse of each finished back tab is spread out and wetted down to stop the rectangle ring from disappearing into the slit. Then on the front side of each back tab add a wisp of fibre through the protruding bar to cover the slit and better secure the bar on that side. Spray and put both back tabs aside.

Step 21: Adding mohair wool yarns

Add mohair wool yarns to the ball, using the usual dunk and place method, in wavy organic lines and slightly overlapping. Aim to cover the area of the ball from the base edge line up to 2.5cm (1in) below the top outside front pocket markings. Avoid covering the two top pocket markings as well as the back tab placement markings.

Step 22: Adding chunky wool yarns

With the ball plug side down in the propping-up bowl, add chunky wool yarns in a spiral pattern from the base centre point to the base edge line. To help secure the spiral during the rest of the layout, take some of the main layer one 25g navy fibre allocation and add a few pieces over the base, covered by thin plastic.

Step 23: Adding silk hankies

Take pieces of silk hankies and/or other embellishment fibres, wisp them out and add them around the top of the ball from the top of the yarns to the top circle line. Extend the fibres up into the C segment in the top circle by up to 5cm (2in) in order to join the fibres up seamlessly with the silk fibres covering the flap. Spray to secure.

Step 24: Adding the outside front pocket 1

On the front of the ball, lift up any silk fibres which are covering the two top pocket markings. Pick up the pocket fibre/template and place it with the front/template flap side facing onto the ball, matching up the four corner markings on the ball with the corners of the template. Spray and smooth the three overlapping edges onto the ball.

Step 25: Adding the outside front pocket 2

Any embellishments such as yarns, which were laid in the front pocket area on the ball, will felt to the front of the pocket. But if any are at the top of the pocket they might end up covered by the template flap. If so, fold out the flap, lift up any yarns onto the front of the pocket fibre, then replace the flap so that it sits against the ball.

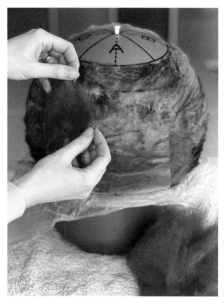

Step 26: Securing the outside front pocket

Fold back down over the top of the pocket template any silk fibres lifted in Step 24. These will be visible on the inside back of the pocket when finished; add further fibres on the template if preferred. To help secure the pocket fibre, add the main layer one 25g red fibre allocation from the top circle line to the middle design line.

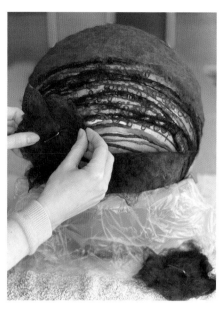

Step 27: Adding the back bottom tabs 1

Peel back the navy fibre at the back of the ball and gently move any yarns out of the way to reveal the bottom tab placement markings. Take the first tab fibre piece and ensure that the rectangle ring lies flat against the tab fibre, with the long bar pointing upwards at the front. Place this against the ball (*see* Step 28 for positioning).

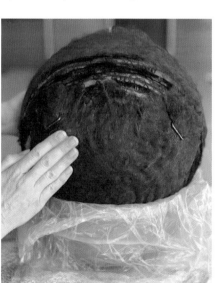

Step 28: Adding the back bottom tabs 2

For the placement of the tab, note that the lower long bar visible on the reverse should match the position of the base edge line and the upper long bar next to the ball should be 2cm (0.75in) above the line. Widthwise the ring should be central to the tab placement marking on the base edge line. Repeat for the second tab.

Step 29: Completing layer one fibre layout

Complete the remaining layer one fibre layout using the rest of the navy fibre to cover the ball as evenly as possible up to the middle design line, ensuring the back bottom tab rings are covered as well as the front outside pocket template. Generously spray the fibre throughout and continue to use plastic to cover the base.

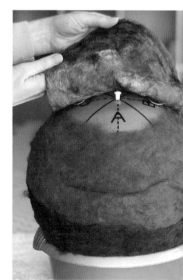

Step 30: Adding the flap 1

Add the flap to the top of the ball, with the decorated/D-ring side facing down. The curved top of each D-ring should meet the B–D area dotted line going across the ball and the top plug should be central to the flap widthwise. When the flap is down, it will extend over the front of the bag by approximately 8cm (3in).

Step 31: Adding the flap 2

The flap will join up with the main fibre across the back and at each side where the B–D area dotted line meets the top circle line. Fluff out the folded side edges of the flap which meet the main fibre. Spray and smooth down those edges and the wispy back edge of the flap so that they are integrated with the rest of the main fibre.

Step 32: Adding the flap 3

The flap is wider than the top circle line, so we need to join the flap at the sides to the main fibre lying beneath it. Use your finger or scissors to lift up the main fibre which is flat to the ball and smooth it against the front of the flap at its edges. Wisp out the join as necessary and spray to secure.

Step 33: Adding the flap 4

Note that the flap joins to the main fibre top edge will now be slightly lifted up and when you lay fibre here in subsequent layers you should maintain the lifted/slightly curved shape. Finally, use scissors to carefully lift any fibres lying flat in the C area of the ball under the flap and smooth them against the flap in that area. Spray.

Step 34: Completing layer two fibre layout

Add the 50g layer two fibre allocation in the usual dunk and place manner and in the same colour configuration as layer one. Aim to cover the initial fibre layout with an even layer all over, including a single thickness of pieces on the flap, right up to the flap edge but not going over. Spray generously with soapy water throughout.

Step 35: Adding the under back pocket fibre

Place the inside back pocket resist template centrally between the bottom rectangle rings, which you can still feel underneath the fibre, with the top of the template lined up with the centre plug. Lift it up and add the 5g (minimum) under inside back pocket fibre allocation under the template for thickness and colour mixing purposes. Reposition the template.

Step 36: Adding the back pocket fibre

Add the 16g inside back pocket fibre allocation on top of the template, starting at the marked line 13cm (5in) below the top edge of the pocket template/plug, in a curve to match the top circle line curve. Overlap the other three template edges with the fibre by at least 2.5cm (1in). Lay out the fibre as evenly as possible all over the template.

Step 37: Completing layer three fibre layout

Add the 50g layer three fibre allocation (I used orange) to complete the fibre layout in the same way as layer two, including over the inside back pocket fibre and a single thickness of pieces on the flap right up to the edge but not going over. Spray and wrap the fibre in plastic. Ensure it lies under the flap with another piece on top.

Step 38: Rubbing the fibre

Place the ball inside the tights, pour on soapy water to ensure the whole ball and tights are soaked, and gently push the ball around in the bowl in all directions, ensuring that the ball makes contact with the sides of the bowl but not pushing so hard that the fibres are moved out of place. Repeat the pushing/rubbing action for 400 pushes.

Step 39: Neatening the edges

Remove the tights and peel back the plastic. Neaten the backpack top edge by fluffing it up, spraying, folding it outwards and gently rubbing. Neaten the pocket edge in the same way. Spray, smooth and lift the flap joins to ensure they keep the same slightly curved position. Replace the plastic and tights.

Step 40: Completing the rubbing

Repeat the push rub action for 400 pushes twice more, making 1,200 in total, pushing more firmly each time. Remove the ball from the tights/plastic after each round, reshape the flap and spray and lift up the flap joins. Spray and rub all folded edges (and around the D-rings if needed) to ensure good fibre bonds and neat shapes.

Step 41: Bouncing the ball

Place the ball in the tights and bounce it on your work surface 500 times. The easiest method is to hold the tights above the ball whilst bouncing. After 500 bounces, remove the tights/plastic to check/rub the edges and reshape the flap. Repeat this process three more times, alternating ball placement in the tights each time.

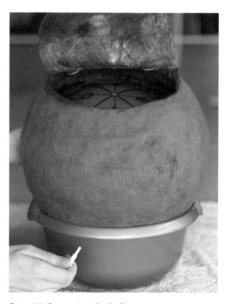

Step 42: Removing the ball

The fibre around the ball should now feel much firmer, tighter and thicker. If not, replace the tights and complete a further round of 500 bounces or more until the fibre is feeling more solid and fully integrated with itself. Remove the tights and plastic, deflate the ball and remove it from the prefelt backpack shape.

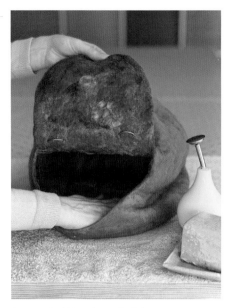

Step 43: Rubbing the embellishments

Give the inside of the backpack a warm soapy shower. Check whether the yarns have felted to the inside by gently running your fingers across them. If they are still moving or not fully adhered, with a very wet and soapy hand do some focused rubbing along the direction they are laid until they are mostly holding in place.

Step 44: Rubbing the outside front pocket

Turn the backpack right side out to check for any further looseness of the yarns/embellishments and continue to rub as needed. Also spend time rubbing the outside front pocket, particularly around the three joining edges, to ensure a tight bond with the main backpack fibre.

Step 45: Rubbing the bottom rings and inside back pocket

Locate and check the two rings on the bottom, which may have sunk into the prefelt. Push (or carefully snip if necessary) the prefelt down around them so they are fully protruding and rub firmly around each ring to anchor them in position. Finally, rub the inside back pocket, particularly the joining edges, to flatten and tighten the fibre.

Step 46: Throwing the backpack

Turn the backpack back to the wrong side and dunk it in warm soapy water. With both hands, loosely pick it up and throw it on the work surface 50 times, spinning the backpack around on its sides as you throw. Then rub the inside embellishments again, the inside and outside pockets and around the bottom rings.

Step 47: Continuing to rub and throw the backpack

Continue to alternate between throwing the backpack in groups of 50 and rubbing all the elements until the backpack is starting to shrink, feel less floppy and the different elements are all feeling firmer. After approximately 250–300 throws in total, turn it right side out and reshape/stretch it. Then flatten it to check and set the orientation.

Step 48: Flattening the backpack

When folded down, the flap should overlap the front pocket by at least 5cm (2in) (if not, stretch the flap) and the D-rings on the flap should be no further forward than the top of the backpack (if they are, scrunch the back area to shrink it down). Then complete 50 flattening throws, flipping it onto alternate sides every ten throws, and reshape.

Step 49: Shaping the backpack

Complete a further 250–300 fulling and shaping actions in total, alternating between stretching the inside, rubbing and patting the outside, using flattening throws, rubbing the pockets and stretching the flap, until the backpack feels thick and sturdy and is keeping its shape. Remove the templates, rinse, towel dry and reshape again.

Step 50: Creating the side folds

If preferred, set small equal folds inwards at the top of each side of the backpack (mine are 5cm/2in down), so that when the flap is closed it completely covers the backpack opening. Secure them with clothes pegs or similar; the indentations can be ironed to remove once dry. Leave the backpack to air dry on a towel.

Step 51: Adding the strap 1

To install a strap (*see* 'Wet Felting a Strap' below for instructions to make a strap), first push each end of the strap through the D-rings on the flap, ensuring the strap is not twisted. Then pass each end through a sliding adjuster ring, so that the central bar is beneath the strap, as shown, leaving at least 25cm (10in) of strap each end.

Step 52: Adding the strap 2

Pass each strap end through the rectangle bar at the bottom of the backpack so that the end folds back under the rest of the strap to meet the reverse of the slider ring. Loosen the strap which is already through the slider ring, to create space to then push the strap end through.

Step 53: Finishing the backpack

Check the fit of the straps and adjust before pulling both parts of the strap through the slider rings to tighten and secure. To attach a turn-lock clasp to the backpack, follow the 'Installing a Turn-Lock Clasp' instructions outlined in Chapter 7.

WET FELTING A STRAP

You'll see a lot of felt cords in wet felting projects, such as a handle for a bag, however there will be scenarios when a cord is too chunky for the project and a flat strap would work much better. The backpack project is a good example of this, as a chunky cord is too thick to work with the metal hardware.

A flat strap might seem like a tricky thing to wet felt, because it involves straight edges, which is always a challenge in wet felting. So I've designed a simple way, using prefelt, of creating a long flat strap which maintains its neat, straight-sided shape, along with being robust enough to use as both a long bag handle and backpack straps. The key, as always with wet felting, is to create a neat layout from the start, and to deploy felting and fulling techniques which won't make the edges wrinkle or become misaligned. It takes quite a lot of flat rubbing and time, but your reward is a perfectly straight felted strap. I've created mine by hand but this is a good instance where a battery-operated sander would be an asset if you use one.

I've used Merino prefelt ribbon as the core of the strap, covered by the same carded wool fibre used for the backpack to add thickness and match its colour. The backpack hardware is 2.5cm (1in) wide, so the finished strap aims to be between 2.2–2.5cm (1in) wide. To achieve this I've used three layers of 2.5cm-wide (1in) Merino prefelt ribbon but as an alternative you could use 10cm (4in) Merino prefelt ribbon or cut a strip this width from any sheet of prefelt, ironed and folded into three to create a 2.5–3cm-wide (1in) strip. The prefelt is then covered with a strip of carded wool fibre. Ideally take a complete strip from a piece of batt, or you can patchwork together pieces of batt fibre as I've done.

Size-wise, although the width shrinkage of the finished strap seems to be fairly consistent between sheep wool fibre breeds (around 2.2–2.5cm/1in in width), I've found the length to be quite variable. For example, the red Finnwool version here started at 150cm (59in) and ended up approximately the same length. Whereas when I've used Bergschaf, as I did for the green variation version, 150cm (59in) as a starting size has more consistently ended up approximately 175cm (69in). Of course there are also variables about how much you stretch the strap during felting and then how much you shrink it down during fulling. Until you've tested the fibre you're using, it's obviously better to err on the side of the strap being too long, which doesn't affect its function, hence I'm recommending a minimum starting size of 150cm (59in). If you don't have a long enough work surface, just work on half or a third of the strap at a time and keep moving it along.

Here are the steps to follow to create a 150cm-long (59in) strap to fit the 25mm (1in) hardware I've used in the backpack project. Simply widen the starting size if you use wider hardware and lengthen it if you would definitely like a longer strap. You could also make a wider strap and attach it to any bag which has integral handle loops or rings, such as the Flap Bag variation project, and use the slider rings along the strap to keep them in place. In addition, in a similar way to the instructions for making a cord at the start of this chapter, you could also make a much shorter and perhaps wider strap and leave the ends unfelted for attaching to a basket or bag.

Step by Step
Laying out the strap

WHAT YOU WILL NEED

Materials
- 450cm × 2.5cm (177in × 1in) length of Merino prefelt ribbon (I used deep pink)
- 150cm × 12cm (59in × 4.5in) (approximately 20g) strip of carded wool fibre (I used red Finnwool)

Equipment
- 190cm × 30cm (75in × 12in) piece of bubble wrap
- 50cm × 50cm (20in × 20in) piece of textured mat
- Washing-up/dishwashing liquid
- Spray bottle containing washing-up liquid and warm water solution
- Rubbing tool
- Cut off leg of tights/pantyhose
- Several small/tea towels
- Scales
- Tape measure
- Small scissors
- Iron and ironing board

Step 1: Collect your prefelt ribbon and carded wool fibre together and ensure a close colour match. Ensure your carded wool strip is an even thickness with wispy edges.

Step 2: Lay the carded wool strip on top of the smooth side of bubble wrap. Measure and cut three 150cm (59in) lengths of prefelt ribbon and lay on top of each other.

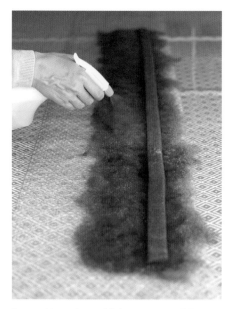

Step 3: Move the prefelt layers on top of the fibre, approximately 2cm (0.75in) from one of the long fibre edges. Spray the fibre and prefelt with soapy water to soak.

Step 4: Using the bubble wrap, fold the long 2cm/0.75in edge of fibre over the long prefelt edge, flatten it down, then fold back the bubble wrap.

Step 5: Use the bubble wrap to turn over the prefelt strip, folding it onto the fibre. Flatten, then fold back the bubble wrap and spray the prefelt to soak.

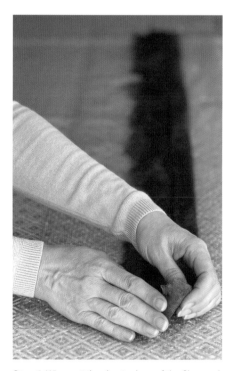

Step 6: Wisp out the short edges of the fibre and fold them over the short edges of the prefelt, smoothing to neaten.

Step 7: Repeat Step 5 until the prefelt has been completely wrapped up in the fibre, spraying throughout to soak. It will expand to approximately 4cm (1.5in) in width.

Felting the strap

Step 8: Wrap up the fibre-covered prefelt strip within the bubble wrap so that each straight edge of the prefelt is against a bubble wrap fold to secure it.

Step 9: Use the rubbing tool to rub along the flat edge of prefelt through the bubble wrap for five minutes. Turn the prefelt over and repeat on the other side. Unwrap the bubble wrap to check the prefelt is still neat and then refold and repeat rubbing for five minutes each side, making 20 minutes in total.

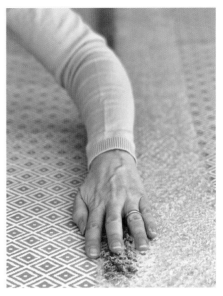

Step 10: Unwrap and check the prefelt strip. It should be starting to feel firmer. Rewrap it in bubble wrap as before and use your hand to rub along the length, with a finger each side to rub along each edge and one on top to rub the flat surface, for five minutes each side, making ten minutes in total.

Step 11: Unwrap and check the prefelt strip. If the surface fibres are no longer moving and the fibre is holding together firmly, repeat Step 10 but rubbing along the fibre directly with your hand for five minutes each side, without the bubble wrap (if not, repeat Step 10 through the bubble wrap again first).

Step 12: During Step 11, alternate rubbing with picking up the strap and gently running it through your hand, which will make it stretch longer (up to 165cm/65in) and become narrower (down to 2.5cm/1in, but avoid it becoming narrower than this). It should start to feel firm and smooth; if not, rub for a further five to ten minutes.

Fulling the strap

Step 13: Rewrap the prefelt in the bubble wrap with a bubble wrap fold snugly against each long edge. Then fold in half and half again so that it is more manageable, place it inside the tights leg to secure and throw it onto the table 100 times. Unwrap to check it and ensure the bubble wrap folds are snug again and throw for a further 100 throws. Throw in total for approximately 5 × 100 throws.

Step 14: If the strap would still benefit from further firming, spend five to ten minutes rubbing it against a textured mat or surface on both the flat and side edges, to fully felt it. Keep an eye on the width throughout to ensure the strap does not get smaller than 2.2–2.5cm (1in) wide. Rubbing the flat sides along the textured mat in the direction of its length will widen it slightly and help to stop it getting too narrow.

Rinsing and finishing

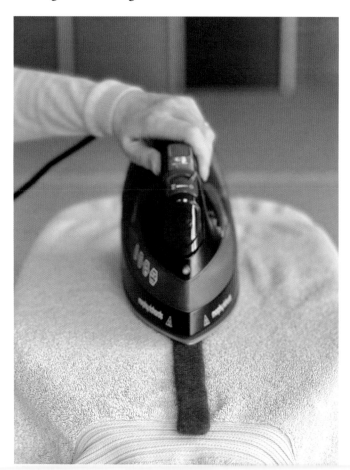

Step 15: Rinse the strap (just squeeze and avoid wringing) in hot and cold water and roll it up in a towel to remove excess water. To give it a final neaten and firm up, rub the strap against a clean textured mat on both the flat and side edges. Leave to air dry and then steam iron to flatten and neaten.

Project Variation

ALTERNATE COLOUR BACKPACKS

Here are two different-coloured versions of the backpack, both created using Bergschaf carded wool batt fibre, along with the red Finnwool one, showing the alternate configurations and strap positions.

Red backpack viewed from the reverse.

Purple and green backpacks configured as shoulder bags, viewed from the front.

Purple backpack viewed from the front.

Green backpack configured as a shoulder bag, viewed from the reverse.

FLAP BAGS

The backpack design easily converts to a less complex bag design, with the same weights, measurements and layout process, but without the outside front pocket or the two sets of rings on the back. Instead, the shoulder or cross-body version (depending on length of strap) has a ring installed at each side of the top edge of the bag, in a similar way to the D-rings installed in the Dartmoor Basket Bag Project, so that we can simply clip on a ready-made bag strap.

Here are two slightly smaller versions of a flap bag, which show different looks you can achieve with the flap. Both use the large purple felting ball at 86.5cm (34in), wool yarn embellishment, 40g of carded wool fibre per layer and a prepared flap size of approximately 25cm high × 16cm wide (10in × 6.25in). The longer purple flap overlapped the top edge by 8cm (3in) during layout, the same as the backpack, and I added a tuck lock clasp to finish; the shorter turquoise flap overlapped by 6cm (2.25in) and I installed a turn-lock clasp. These are slight differences and are the sort of details you can tinker with in your designs until you create your preferred look. Note that I also reduced the amount of fibre per layer compared to the backpack, which is deliberately sturdier structurally.

Turquoise bag made from Corriedale carded wool sliver with a slightly shorter flap and turn-lock clasp.

Purple bag made from MC-1 carded wool batt fibre with a longer flap and tuck lock clasp.

Reverse of the purple bag, showing the yarn design and changed overall shape compared to the backpack, due to the different ring placement.

CAT CAVE PROJECT

I've been keen to create a cat cave design on a ball for a while, but have been hampered by the challenging requirement for a much larger starting size ball. This is where an exercise ball has turned out to be the ideal solution, because they come in a range of much larger sizes, they inflate and deflate easily via a plug and are made of durable, thick rubber as they need to be strong enough for a person to sit on safely. After a bit of experimentation, I've found a 45cm (height) exercise ball which has been perfect for the task.

With the ball sorted, going large then brings challenges in terms of managing the size: we still need tights and a rubbing bowl to fit, and the felting process becomes more of a physical effort. However, the cat cave project uses a simple layout, with no additional embellishment other than a pair of ears! The ears are created from two separate book resists made of triangle-shaped foam. At its simplest, a book resist is a flat 2D flap-like template around which you add fibre, like the page of a book, to achieve a 3D element. So, by attaching a triangle-shaped resist to the ball, we can create a hollow extra shape of fibre resembling a cat's ear. I've created a base flap at the bottom of the resist templates for attaching, which I've scored with scissors so that it bends. Packing tape seemed to work best at attaching them to the ball, without being permanent.

Because we are using the ear resists attached to the ball, it's much easier to work right side out with the fibre layout. So this is the only project where layer one is the inside colour and layer three is the outside fibre colour. I used Shetland carded wool sliver, deliberately using three different but complementary colours for each layer apart from the ears, which I kept darker. This keeps the layout simple to keep track of and is a good example of colour mixing, using three similar, natural, animal-like colours to create a blended, slightly variegated result, which more resembles animal fur colour. So my choice of fibre was very much dictated by the animal colours I wanted to use, but you can use any carded wool fibre or colour combination you prefer. If you're like me, once you make one you'll start getting lots of ideas for different animal versions, and the ears are easily adaptable to other shapes. But you'll see I was inspired to make a cat-style cat cave based on my own cats, who have pointed (darker) ears.

WHAT YOU WILL NEED

Materials
- Approximately 300g of carded wool fibre in your chosen colours: 100g per main layer (×3)
- I used Shetland carded wool sliver fibre in the following combination:

Layout Element	Colour	Amount
Layer 1	Dark grey	90g
Ears (×2)	Dark grey	10g (5g each)
Layer 2	Light grey	90g
Ears (back, ×2)	Dark grey	6g (3g each)
Ears (front, ×2)	Light grey	4g (2g each)
Layer 3	Natural white	90g
Ears (back, ×2)	Dark grey	6g (3g each)
Ears (front, ×2)	Light grey	4g (2g each)

Equipment
- Extra large yellow ball, inflated to 117cm (46in) circumference
- Inflating pump
- 5–6mm (0.25in) thick foam ear resist templates (*see* Chapter 8, Templates and Tables)
- 32cm (12.5in) minimum internal diameter round bowl to prop up the ball
- Large bowl of any size to hold the washing-up liquid and warm water solution
- 43cm (17in) minimum external diameter tub to push rub the ball within
- Two pairs of XXL (137–152cm/54–60in hips) tights/pantyhose, 20 denier (*see* Chapter 1 for preparation)
- Two 100cm × 55cm (40in × 22in) pieces of thin plastic
- Washing-up/dishwashing liquid
- Olive oil soap
- Spray bottle containing washing-up liquid and warm water solution
- Ball brause
- Several large towels
- Several small/tea towels
- Scales
- Tape measure
- Ruler
- Permanent marker pen
- Large general-purpose scissors
- Packing tape or other strong tape

I haven't marked up the ball because of the simple layout, but you could mark guidelines for the opening and ears if you prefer: with the ball inflated to 117cm (46in) in circumference, the top circle line is 9cm (3.5in) out from the centre plug, making a circle diameter of 18cm (7in); the bottom edge of each ear is 20cm (8in) from the centre plug and the ears start 13cm (5in) apart.

The finished cat cave weighs approximately 300g and measures approximately 36cm wide × 31cm high and 104cm in circumference (14in × 12in, 41in in circumference).

Step by Step

Step 1: Assembling and preparing your materials

Collect your carded wool fibre together to create a pleasing colour palette. Weigh out all fibre in your chosen colours for each of the three layers, and keep each layer and the ear fibre allocations for each layer separate. Tear all fibre into palm-sized pieces. Inflate the felting ball to 117cm (46in) in circumference.

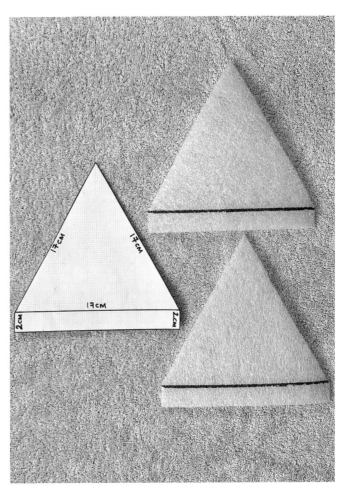

Step 2: Preparing the ear resists

Use the ear template to create two triangle-shaped foam resists. Note that each has a 2cm (0.75in) base flap for attaching to the felting ball. Mark the 2cm (0.75in) line and gently score along it with scissors and a ruler so that it bends, taking care not to cut completely through the resist. Repeat for the second ear resist.

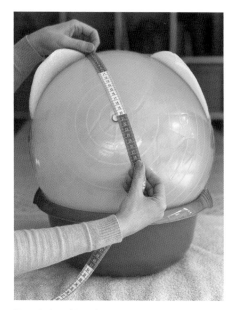

Step 3: Attaching the ear resists part 1

Use strong tape to attach the base flap of each ear resist to the ball. The marked line of each ear resist should be 20cm (8in) out from the centre of the plug. Note that this ball has concentric circle lines marked around it which helps with the placement, but you could mark the 20cm (8in) circle line around the ball if preferred.

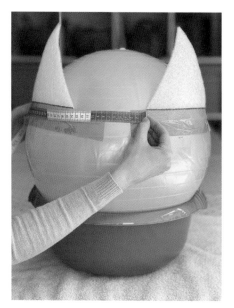

Step 4: Attaching the ear resists part 2

The ear resists should be placed 13cm (5in) apart. Note that the tape covers the area beneath the back of the ears (rather than the front of the ears) to encourage the ears to be bending slightly forwards when the cat cave is finished, to give a more natural cat-like look.

Step 5: Layer one main fibre layout

Using the 90g fibre allocation for layer one, take a piece of the dark grey fibre, dunk it in soapy water, ensure it is spread out and completely soaked and place it directly on top of the back of the ball. Repeat to cover the back and base of the ball with an initial layer of fibre, using around half the layer's fibre allocation at this stage.

Step 6: Layer one ear fibre layout

Using the 5g ear fibre allocation for each ear, cover the front and back of each ear resist evenly with the fibre, dunking and placing it as usual. Ensure the fibre is tight around all sides and edges of each resist, and ensure there is plenty of fibre around the base of each resist where it joins the ball.

Step 7: Finishing layer one fibre layout

Continue Step 5 to complete the rest of the main fibre layout. Leave an opening circle free of fibre (you could mark the circle on the ball first if preferred) which is 9cm (3.5in) out from the centre plug, making an opening circle diameter of 18cm (7in). Cover the rest of the ball with an initial layer of fibre and then infill thinner areas.

Step 8: Layer two fibre layout

Repeat the fibre layout with the light grey layer two fibre allocation, starting with the ear fibre. Note that I used light grey on the front of the ear resist/inside of the ears and dark grey on the sides and back of the resist to create darker ears. Use the full fibre allocation to cover the entire ball up to the opening circle as evenly as possible.

Step 9: Layer three fibre layout

Repeat Step 8 to complete the layout with the natural white layer three fibre. Note that the layer three ear fibre allocation and placement is exactly the same as layer two. Add any extra fibre you feel necessary to thicken thin areas, and with soapy hands give the ears a gentle rub to ensure the fibre feels tight around the resists.

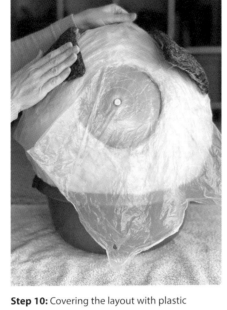

Step 10: Covering the layout with plastic

Lay a small piece of plastic between the ears and the front of the main fibre and gently push the ears forward onto it so that they do not felt to the rest of the cat cave. Generously spray the fibre all over and wrap in plastic.

Step 11: Preparing to rub the fibre

Stretch one pair of tights over the large tub, place the ball inside so that the plug and opening are covered and gently pull up the edges of the tights as high as they will go. Repeat with the second pair of tights, this time placing the ball inside so that the area not covered by the first pair is covered.

Step 12: Rubbing the fibre

Place the ball inside the tub, pour on soapy water to ensure the whole ball and tights are soaked, and gently push the ball around the tub in all directions, ensuring that the ball makes contact with the sides of the tub but not pushing so hard that the fibres are moved out of place. Repeat the pushing/rubbing action for 400 pushes.

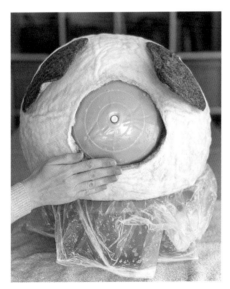

Step 13: Neatening the opening edge and ears

Peel each pair of tights away from the ball and back over the edges of the tub, and place the ball on the propping-up bowl. Peel back the plastic to reveal the opening edge. Neaten it all around by fluffing up the edge, folding it outwards, spraying and gently rubbing. With soapy hands, rub the ears to tighten the fibre around the resists.

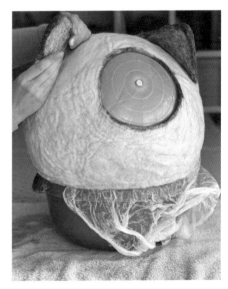

Step 14: Completing the rubbing

Replace the plastic and tights and repeat the push rub action for 400 pushes twice more, pushing more firmly each time. Remove the ball from the tights/plastic after each round, then spray and rub the opening edge and ears to neaten the edge and ensure the fibre around the ear resists feels tight and increasingly firm.

Step 15: Bouncing the ball

Place the ball in the tights and bounce it on your work surface 500 times. The easiest method is to hold the tights above the ball whilst bouncing. After 500 bounces, remove the tights/plastic to check/rub the edges and ears as before. Repeat this process at least twice more, alternating ball placement in the tights each time.

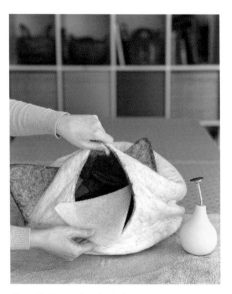

Step 16: Removing the ball

The fibre around the ball should now feel much firmer, tighter and thicker. If not, replace the tights and complete a further round of 500 bounces or more until the fibre feels more solid and fully integrated with itself. Remove the tights/plastic, deflate the ball and remove it from the prefelt cat cave shape, along with the ear resists.

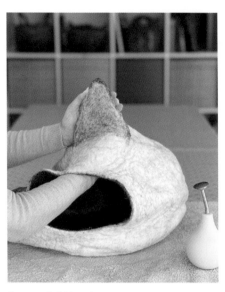

Step 17: Rubbing the ears

Give your hands and the ears a good soapy shower. Spend some time rubbing the ears, with one hand inside to hold the shape and one hand outside to rub the sides and edges, until they feel quite firm and are holding their shape well. Fill a bowl with warm soapy water and dunk the whole cat cave in the water to soak it.

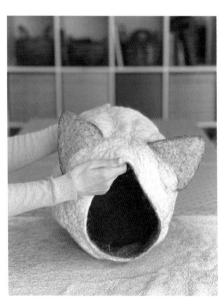

Step 18: Throwing the cat cave

Loosely pick up the cat cave and throw it on the work surface 100 times, spinning it around on its sides as you throw and maintaining the rounded shape at all times. After 100 throws, reshape it and rub the ears. Continue to throw in groups of 100, alternating with rubbing the ears, until it feels thicker, firmer and is holding its shape.

Step 19: Rinsing the cat cave

Rinse the cat cave under warm running water, or soak in bowls of warm water, squeezing gently until the water runs clear. Alternate between hot and cold water rinses if the felt still needs firming. Remove excess water by rolling the cat cave up in a dry towel. Clean the ball of soap, reinsert and inflate it as large as possible

Step 20: Finishing the cat cave

Leave the cat cave to air dry on a towel. Before it is completely dry, remove the ball and flatten the bottom area inside with your hand to create a flat base to enable the cat cave to stay in place better. Then, once completely dry, just fill with cat and enjoy!

FOX CAVE

I also created a fox version of the cat cave. The placement measurements and fibre amounts are all the same as the main cat version. To create the fox colouring I used 100g of Corriedale carded wool sliver in each of three complementary beige and red brown animal shades, with Fox for the final outside layer. For the ear colours I used the main layer colour for the back and sides of the ears but used Fawn for all the front inside ear layouts, as shown.

Layer one (Fawn) fibre layout.

Layer two (Chestnut Chap) fibre layout with Fawn front inside ears.

Layer three (Fox) fibre layout with Fawn front inside ears.

Layer three (Fox) fibre layout showing Fox back of the ears.

CHAPTER 5

NUNO FELTING ON A BALL

uno or laminated felt are terms used to describe the technique of felting wool fibre to fabric (*Nuno* is the Japanese word for cloth). It's an amazing technique for adding pattern and texture to felt.

In the initial felting stage, the wool fibre bonds to the fabric by grabbing hold of it and migrating through the tiny holes in the fabric. Then once the process moves on to the fulling stage, because the fabric does not have the properties to shrink it gets pulled into a smaller surface area by the shrinking of the felt. This causes the fabric to ruche up into attractive patterns and create interesting textures. Once fully bonded, the felt and fabric become a new combined, laminated fabric, with felt on one side and fabric on the other.

There are different ways of using the nuno felting technique, from bonding a complete layer of fabric to the felt to incorporating small pieces, or even using a whole piece of fabric and adding fibre to just a few areas. The advantage of using a complete layer is that it brings extra strength to the finished felt, so it is often used to create very fine, drapey felt using a thin layer of Merino wool fibre and silk fabric. This combination works particularly well for garments, scarves and other items which will be worn next to the skin, as they are soft, flexible and lightweight yet very strong. However, you don't just have to nuno felt with fine materials, you can also combine fabric with coarser wool fibre, and it works just as well with felting on a ball as flat felting.

This chapter includes three very different nuno felting on a ball projects to give you some ideas about how you can use this technique, ranging from partial use of fabric pieces to a complete layer, and very sturdy felting to very fine. Before we get started on those, let's cover some basics about the process plus some tips for successful nuno felting on a ball.

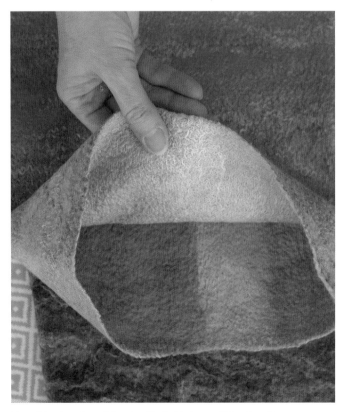

Nuno felted cowl scarf showing the inside layer of Margilan silk.

NUNO FELTING MATERIALS

We already know how to add a range of surface design materials to our felt from the projects in the previous chapters, and using fabric is no different. Nuno felting uses the same principle of laying fabric next to wool fibre and felting them together using the same wet felting techniques. The key to its success, however, is using the right fabric in the first place. Ideally you want to use a fabric which is either very fine or has a very open weave so you can see the tiny holes between the warp and weft lines. Silk is a very popular choice, in particular Margilan silk from Uzbekistan, which is incredibly fine (rarefied/scrim is the finest), felts quickly and also brings a beautiful sheen to the finished felt. You can also use other silks, like silk chiffon and sari silk, as well as open weave fabrics such as cotton scrim, cheesecloth, lace and net, basically anything which has visible holes in it. Any wool fibre will work with nuno felting, although it is most commonly used with Merino due to its fineness.

Variety of patterned sari silk fabric and metallic ribbons.

Delicate, hand-dyed Margilan silk fabrics showing their open weave structure.

Sequined fabric, consisting of sequins on a net base.

NUNO FELTING ON A BALL

When nuno felting, we add the fabric pieces to the ball first, as we do with most embellishment materials, to protect our layout, using either the dunk and place or spraying methods, depending how easy your fabric is to handle when wet. Fabric works particularly well on the ball because, once wet, it stays put even when you're moving the ball around. We then add the wool fibre on top and follow the usual felting on a ball process.

One of the main concepts to follow with nuno felting is that we need to be careful not to felt the fibre before it has fully bonded with the fabric. So as a general rule you would want to take the initial felting stage a little slower by using cooler water to ensure that heat does not play a part, which is consistent with how we work on the felting ball. Another key aspect is to disrupt the close placement of the fibres and fabric as little as possible by being less hands-on whilst agitating the fibre. This is why an electric sander is often used in nuno felting as it keeps everything in place whilst also providing agitation through vibration. Using the felting ball works well for the hands-off aspect, as generally we don't directly put our hands on the fibre/fabric until prefelt stage when we remove the ball. And the natural compacting process of pushing the fibre tightly against the ball (with the fabric sandwiched in between) during the push rub stage helps the fabric and fibre to stay in place whilst still being agitated. Nuno felting is therefore a technique which is well suited to felting on a ball.

USEFUL TIPS WHEN NUNO FELTING

Here are some extra tips I usually follow when nuno felting on the ball.

Hands-Off Agitation

As a general rule, during the felting stage we're going to complete the full three rounds of 400 push rubs and full four rounds of 500 bounces (except the Silk Cowl Project, because the Margilan silk and fine layer of Merino felts so fast). The reason for this is that, because we want to be hands-off from our fabric for as long as possible, there's no advantage in completing less rounds of bouncing and then stopping to remove the ball so we can give the inside a rub, which we want to avoid. We want to give the fabric as much time as possible on its own to felt with the fibre, and ideally not rub it at all with our hands directly during the early stages, which has more potential for displacing it. So it is generally better to do four rounds or more of bouncing, and more push rubs if things aren't feeling firm after three rounds. There might also be occasions when you might remove the ball, check how well the fabric has bonded and, if it would benefit from more hands-off agitation, soak the inside, re-inflate the ball and continue push rubs/bouncing.

Throw Gently

During the fulling stage, once you have removed the ball, start throwing very gently initially until you know the fabric is fully bonding with the felt. Throwing the felt is still a great technique for encouraging bonding, but we want to do it slowly and less forcefully until much later in the fulling/shaping/shrinking stages than usual once we know that the fibre and fabric have bonded.

Careful Stitching

If you find that some of your fabrics still aren't bonding, avoid needle felting them as this will destroy the fabric. Instead, try adding a few small stitches to hold them down, or trim them. If you make any adjustments like this at prefelt stage you're unlikely to notice them by the end.

Let's get started with our first nuno felting project, which involves creating a design with a simple shape of fabric.

SPARKLE STAR BAG PROJECT

For this first nuno felting project we're using nuno elements rather than a complete layer of fabric. Using sequined fabric (which comprises sequins on a net base) is a great way of incorporating a hard shiny object (like a sequin) which wouldn't normally felt in, but because it is attached to net fabric (which *will* felt in) we can adhere it securely that way. The contrast between sparkly fabric and matte wool felt is a really striking one. The star of the show here is (literally) the sparkly sequined star.

So in terms of surface design this is very simple. I was inspired by the star bag strap to create this project and, as the strap is very busy, the bag seemed to only need a simple design.

Structure-wise this is a different bag design to try. We're still felting in metal rings to clip the strap onto but this time they are on the outside of the bag and can be any size or shape. There's no flap closure so this leaves the top opening of the bag uninterrupted by the rings or a flap, which allows us to easily insert a zip. I know zips are often a bit of a mystery to inexperienced sewers (me included), but this is really simple to install

WHAT YOU WILL NEED

Materials
- Approximately 140g of carded wool fibre in your chosen colours: 3g per ring tab (×2); and 45g per main layer (×3)
- I used Finnwool carded wool batt fibre in the following combination:

Layout Element	Colour	Amount
Ring tabs (×2)	Dark green	6g (3g each)
Layer 1	Dark green	45g
Layer 2	Dark green	45g
Layer 3	Bright green	45g

- 40cm × 20cm (16in × 8in) piece of sequined fabric (I used bright pink)
- Two metal rings (I used 30mm × 20mm gold rectangle rings)
- 140cm (55in) adjustable and detachable cross-body bag strap with metal lobster clasp (or similar) ends
- 30cm (12in) zip (I used dark green)
- Sewing thread to match the zip (I used dark green)

Equipment
For the wet felting
- Large purple felting ball, inflated to 89cm (35in) circumference
- Inflating pump
- Star template (*see* Chapter 8, Templates and Tables)
- 25cm (10in) internal diameter round bowl or similar to prop up the ball
- Large bowl of any size to hold the washing-up liquid and warm water solution
- 32cm (12.5in) minimum internal diameter round or square bowl to push rub the ball within
- Two pairs of XXL (137–152cm/54-60in hips) tights/pantyhose, 20 denier (*see* Chapter 1 for preparation)
- 100cm × 55cm (40in × 22in) piece of thin plastic
- 25cm × 25cm (10in × 10in) piece of bubble wrap
- Washing-up/dishwashing liquid
- Olive oil soap
- Spray bottle (containing washing-up liquid and warm water solution)
- Ball brause
- Several large towels
- Several small/tea towels
- Scales
- Tape measure
- Ruler
- Pen or pencil
- Small and large scissors

For sewing the zip
- Pins
- Sewing needle
- Scissors

by hand whilst still being perfectly strong (*see* Chapter 7 for full instructions). I've shaped the bag to make it quite rounded but you could make it much flatter if you prefer or even shape it to have a completely round profile. I rather like the curved top of the bag which has resulted from having the two top edges so close during layout, which creates a different look.

To keep things simple, I've used just two colours of green Finnwool for this project – as usual, any carded wool fibre would work fine: two layers of dark green on the outside and middle layers of the bag, and bright green on the inside. I haven't included a pocket in order to avoid risking distorting one of the sides and hence the star design, but obviously you could include one in the same way I've shown you in the Chapter 4 projects.

The finished bag weighs approximately 170g including metal rings and zip and measures approximately 27cm wide × 22cm high × 14cm deep and 66cm in circumference (10.5in × 8.75in × 5.5in, 26in in circumference).

Step by Step

Step 1: Assembling and preparing your materials

Collect your carded wool fibre and sequined fabric together to create a pleasing colour palette. Weigh 45g of wool batt fibre in your chosen colours for each of the three layers, and 2 × 3g amounts for the ring tabs. Tear all fibre into palm-sized pieces and keep separate. Inflate the felting ball to 89cm (35in) in circumference.

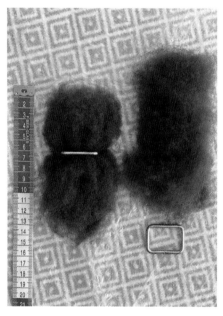

Step 2: Preparing the first ring tab part 1

Take each 3g ring tab fibre allocation and layer it up into an approximate rectangle measuring 14cm × 6cm (5.5in × 2.5in). Pass one fibre pile through the first ring so that the ring sits centrally on the fibre, with the ring oriented landscape-style if using rectangle rings.

Step 3: Preparing the first ring tab part 2

With the first ring and fibre lying on bubble wrap, spray the fibre to soak it. Carefully pick up the ring by the top bar and fold down each side of the fibre to meet the other, so that the lower bar of the ring is sandwiched at the fibre fold. Wisp out the sides of the fibre below the bar to create a single integrated piece of fibre.

Step 4: Preparing the first ring tab part 3

Take four pieces of fibre from the layer one allocation and layer them on top of the ring tab fibre, overlapping the edges each side. Spray and smooth them down all over, including just over the fibre fold, to fully integrate them with the original ring tab fibre. This extra fibre will help integrate the ring tab fibre with the main bag fibre.

Step 5: Preparing the second ring tab

Repeat Steps 2–4 for the second ring tab and put both aside. Keep them oriented with the additional fibre side facing upwards. This is the side which will need to face the ball when you start the main layout.

Step 6: Preparing the stars

Use a card or paper template to cut out two large star shapes from the sequined fabric. Cut as neatly as possible as the edges will be visible in the finished bag. Bear in mind that you will be cutting sequins so the ones on the edges will break and fall off.

Step 7: Adding the first star

With the felting ball plug side up on the propping-up bowl, first spray the surface to help the stars stick. Place the first star on the ball, with the sequined side facing the ball, oriented between the top design line and the base edge line and with the centre of the star lined up with the dotted placement line at B. Spray to secure in place.

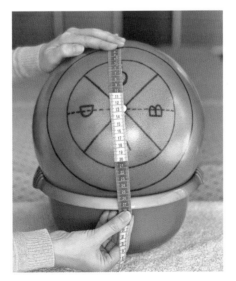

Step 8: Adding the second star

Repeat for the second star, lining it up on the opposite side of the ball and with the star central to the dotted placement line at D. Note that you will now be completely covering the ball with fibre except leaving a thin 25.5cm (10in) opening along the dotted placement lines at A and C and extending to the top design line each side.

Step 9: Adding the first ring tab

Take the first ring tab, dunk it in soapy water and place it on the ball with the additional fibre side facing the ball. The top visible bar of the ring should be in line with the top design line, with the centre of the ring lined up with the dotted placement line at C. Smooth out all the wispy fibre edges.

Step 10: Securing the first ring tab

Using some of the 45g fibre allocation for layer one, take a piece of the dark green fibre, dunk it in soapy water, ensure it is spread out and completely soaked and place it directly on top of the first ring tab. Repeat to cover the ring tab all over, including the visible part of the ring, to help secure it in place.

Step 11: Securing the second ring tab

Continue to put a layer of fibre all around the rest of the ball until you reach the side of the ball in the A area. Then repeat Step 9 to add the second ring tab, lining up the centre of the ring with the dotted placement line at A. Add fibre on top as in Step 10 and then all over the rest of the ball, except the thin opening outlined in Step 8.

Step 12: Completing layer one and two fibre layouts

Complete the first layer of fibre all over, infilling any thinner areas until the layer one fibre is all used. Then repeat with the 45g layer two fibre allocation, adding fibre as evenly as you can all over the ball and again up to the narrow top opening, patting regularly to check evenness. Add extra fibre as necessary to thicken any thin areas.

Step 13: Adding layer three fibre

Repeat Step 12 with the 45g layer three fibre allocation (I used bright green). Once added, check that the edges of the opening are wispy and there is a gap between edges; adjust as necessary. Generously spray the fibre all over and wrap in plastic.

Step 14: Preparing to rub the fibre

Stretch one pair of tights over the 32cm (12.5in) internal diameter rubbing bowl, place the ball inside and gently pull up the edges of the tights as high as they will go. Repeat with the second pair, this time placing the ball inside so that the area not covered by the first pair is covered. Pour on soapy water to soak the tights.

Step 15: Rubbing the fibre

Place the ball inside the bowl and gently push the ball around the bowl in all directions, ensuring that the ball makes contact with the sides of the bowl but not pushing so hard that the fibres are moved out of place. Repeat the pushing/rubbing action for 400 pushes.

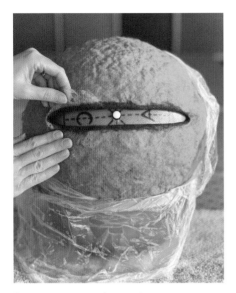

Step 16: Neatening the opening

Peel each pair of tights away from the ball and back over the edges of the bowl, and place the ball on the propping-up bowl. Peel back the plastic to reveal the fibre opening. Neaten the opening all around by fluffing up the edges, folding them outwards, spraying and gently rubbing to secure. Replace the plastic and tights.

Step 17: Completing the rubbing

Repeat the push rub action for 400 pushes twice more, pushing more firmly each time. Remove the ball from the tights/plastic after each round, soaking the fibre as necessary. Also spray and rub the opening edges to ensure the folded edges integrate well with the main fibre. Note that the opening edges will start to recede.

Step 18: Bouncing the ball

Place the ball in the tights and bounce it on your work surface 500 times. The easiest method is to hold the tights above the ball whilst bouncing. After 500 bounces, remove the tights/plastic to check/rub the opening edges as before. Repeat this process at least three more times, alternating ball placement in the tights each time.

Step 19: Removing the ball

The fibre around the ball should now feel much firmer, tighter and thicker. If not, replace the tights and complete a further round of 500 bounces or more until the fibre is feeling more solid and fully integrated with itself. Remove the tights and plastic, deflate the ball and remove it from the prefelt bag shape.

Step 20: Rubbing the ring tabs

Give the inside of the bag a good soapy shower but try not to rub inside at this stage to avoid disrupting the stars. Soak the ring tabs and spend a few minutes rubbing around each with very wet and soapy hands to adhere the tabs fully to the outside of the bag and shrink and firm the fibre holding the rings.

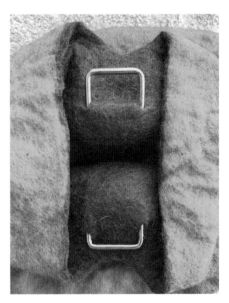

Step 21: Firming the ring tabs

Note that the fibre around the upper ring tab shown, which has been rubbed, is much firmer around the metal ring, particularly the non-visible bar of the ring. In comparison, the fibre around the lower ring tab shown is still loose around the non-visible bar of the ring as this has not yet been rubbed to firm it.

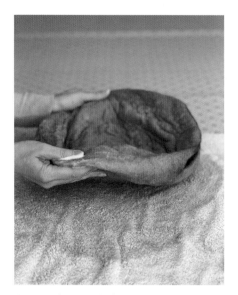

Step 22: Throwing the bag

With the bag still inside out, slightly flatten it down on its main sides, oriented with the rings left and right. Gently throw the two main sides of the bag down on the work surface, for ten throws on each side before alternating, up to 100 throws. The purpose is to gently encourage the felt to shrink and adhere fully to the fabric stars.

Step 23: Shaping and stretching

Check the stars are adhering to the felt. If not, soak the inside of the bag, replace the ball and rub the area of the stars from outside with your hands, completing further bouncing as necessary. If they are adhering well, put your hands inside and stretch and rub the main sides to start shaping the bag. Repeat Step 22 for a further 100 throws.

Step 24: Shaping the bag

The felt should be starting to shrink, feel thicker and develop a crinkled texture. Turn the bag right side out, reshape and then repeat a further 200 throws in the same way as Step 22, alternating between gentle throwing, stretching the inside to shape the bag and rubbing all over with soapy hands to smooth out the wrinkles on the surface.

Step 25: Rinsing the bag

Rinse the bag under warm running water, or soak in bowls of warm water, squeezing gently until the water runs clear. Alternate between hot and cold water rinses if the felt still needs firming. Remove excess water by rolling the bag up in a dry towel, then reshape (I used a small cushion to stuff mine) and leave to air dry on a towel.

Step 26: Installing the zip

Using the instructions in Chapter 7, install a zip into the bag opening. As the zip will take a lot of wear, once you have sewn the zip with one row of sewing stitches (and checked its fit and look from the outside), go over the stitching again in the gaps between stitches to create a back-stitch effect for strength.

Step 27: Finishing the bag

You might also want to neaten the zip inside by adding a lining to, or sewing down, the edges of the zip. Otherwise, turn your bag the right side out, zip up the bag and attach a matching strap to finish.

SARI SILK BOWL PROJECT

We're returning to a bowl shape for our next nuno felting project, which uses pieces of sari silk as our primary surface embellishment and aims to show how you can bring together lots of fabric scraps to create a cohesive design. I've pulled together different materials within largely the same colour palette (reds and dark purples), including not just patterned sari silk fabric but also sari silk glitter ribbon, cotton scrim, lace, chunky yarn and silk caps. I've combined these with a 100g braid of hand-dyed Corriedale combed wool tops in similar colours. So part of the fun of this project is collecting materials together and using up scraps from your stash.

The broad bowl shape gives a big surface area to display all the different materials and textures. Key to success with this project is using very feltable embellishments, so ideally use materials you already know will felt well. The order you add materials to the ball doesn't have to be the same as mine, but as we're adding a lot of different materials we need to be mindful of overlapping. So avoid overlapping any of the fabric, which doesn't have the properties to felt, but as wool yarn is feltable you can add it on top of the fabric. Silk fibres won't felt on their own, but if they are very wispy the main wool fibre can get through them to bond with the fabrics so you can also put those on top.

I started by laying out embellishments on the base, but that was just so that I had the largest surface area to work with. I used a combination of placing and spraying for any delicate embellishments, such as the Margilan silk and silk caps, and dunking and placing for the sari silk fabric pieces, yarns and wool fibre. You can either prepare fabrics in advance or cut as you go as I did.

I used hand-dyed Corriedale combed wool tops for this project (as I did for the Hanging Basket Set in Chapter 4), which kept its structure well enough to dunk and place on the ball. I still prepared pieces in advance by pulling off palm-sized wisps. As I used the same fibre for all three layers, to differentiate between them during layout I divided up the colours and used the deeper red and purple colours for layers one and three and kept the lighter colours in layer two.

This bowl is a little different as I've included a small rim around the top edge. If you'd like a much larger rim, just use the same technique I've shown you but extend the fibre (*see* Step 11). You could also add extra surface design elements like curly locks extending from the rim, or differently shaped structural pieces. An important point to remember is that extra structural elements like a rim, which aren't constrained from shrinking by being held in place by the felting ball, will shrink and felt much more quickly than the rest of the item. So the 5cm (2in) of extending fibre for the rim during layout turned into just a 1.5cm (0.5in) rim by the end. Add more fibre to the length of the extension if you would like a bigger rim. But keep the rim fibre

Materials

- Approximately 100g of carded wool fibre in your chosen colours: 33g per main layer (×3) (I used a 100g braid of hand-dyed Corriedale combed wool tops in reds and purples)
- A selection of small pieces of sari and other silk fabric, cut into strips measuring approximately 5cm × 10cm (2in × 4in) (I used sari silk, Margilan silk and silk chiffon)
- Any other embellishment materials preferred (I used sari silk glitter ribbon, cotton scrim, lace, chunky yarn and silk caps)

Equipment

- Large purple felting ball, inflated to 80cm (31.5in) circumference
- Green felting ball, inflatable to 65cm (25.5in) circumference
- Inflating pump
- Small round bowl to prop up the ball
- Large bowl of any size to hold the washing-up liquid and warm water solution
- 28cm (11in) minimum internal diameter round or square bowl to push rub the ball within
- Two pairs of medium/large (102–122cm/40–48in hips) tights/pantyhose, 20 denier (*see* Chapter 1 for preparation)
- 100cm × 55cm (40in × 22in) piece of thin plastic
- Second smaller piece of plastic
- Washing-up/dishwashing liquid
- Olive oil soap
- Spray bottle (containing washing-up liquid and warm water solution)
- Ball brause
- Several large towels
- Several small/tea towels
- Scales
- Tape measure
- Small scissors

layout, and particularly the area where the join/fold lies at the top edge circle line, slightly thinner to compensate for the faster shrinkage and thickening of the rim/rim join.

We'll be checking and smoothing the rim fibre after each round of felting to ensure it doesn't get thick and lumpy. Bear in mind that, when we neaten the edge after the first push rub round, we'll be folding the fluffed-up fibre edge *inwards* (rather than outwards like normal). This is because the rim is an extension of the inside colour of the bowl (layer three) and curves downwards slightly, so when it's finished we see a different side of it at the edge than usual.

I've also included a brimmed hat variation version which aims to showcase all things sari silk: not just sari silk fabric, but also sari silk yarn and sari silk fibre blends. It also has a slightly larger and more prominent brim. So structurally this project is very versatile in that you can create items as diverse as a hat or bowl using exactly the same starting materials and measurements, although note my points about size in the variation project below.

The finished bowl weighs approximately 125g and measures approximately 20cm wide × 19cm high (8in × 7.5in), and 65cm (25.5in) in circumference.

Step by Step

Step 1: Assembling and preparing your embellishment materials

Collect a variety of embellishment materials together to create a pleasing colour palette. Cut your silk fabric pieces into strips measuring 5cm × 10cm (2in × 4in) on average, including longer strips up to 20cm (8in) and other shapes if preferred. Note that ironing your fabrics first makes them easier to cut.

Step 2: Preparing your wool fibre/equipment

Weigh 33g of wool fibre in your chosen colours for each of the three layers (I used a hand-dyed combed wool tops braid). Tear or wisp all fibre into palm-sized pieces. Inflate the felting ball to 80cm (31.5in) in circumference and place it upside down on the propping-up bowl. Spray the ball with soapy water to start.

Step 3: Adding the silk pieces

First add sari silk pieces to the ball, dunking them in soapy water, laying them in different directions and keeping them as flat and unfolded/uncreased as possible. Then add any very lightweight, sheer silk fabrics, such as Margilan and chiffon, which you can lay flat or scrunch up before spraying to secure.

Step 4: Adding other fabric embellishments

Add further fabric embellishments, such as ribbons, lace and cotton scrim, using either the dunk and place method or spraying in place if more lightweight and delicate. Keep all the pieces spread out and not overlapping, and ensure that there are still plenty of gaps between embellishments.

Step 5: Adding wool yarns

Continue to build up a pleasing design by soaking and adding wool yarn in a random wiggly path all over the ball, aiming to fill in gaps in the embellishments but also overlapping some. Also add short lengths of chunky wool yarns to vary the design. Ensure that none of the embellishments go beyond the top edge circle line.

Step 6: Adding embellishment fibres

Finally, add any embellishment or lustre fibres, such as silk caps or hankies. Tear apart the layers of fibres and cut pieces from one of the layers. Spread and wisp these apart with your fingers and then place on the ball, spraying to secure. Once you're happy with the overall surface coverage, move on to the next step.

Step 7: Layer one wool fibre layout

Using the 33g fibre allocation for layer one, take a piece of the fibre, dunk it in soapy water, ensure it is spread out and completely soaked and place it directly on top of the fibres anywhere on the ball. Repeat to cover the whole ball and just going over the top circle line, without using up all the fibre allocation at this stage.

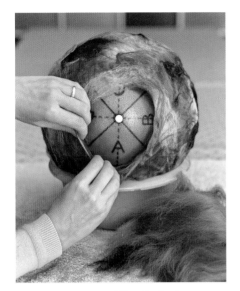

Step 8: Laying out wool fibre for the rim

Working at the top of the ball, extend the fibre layout to at least 4cm (1.5in) from the top edge circle line. Then put your fingers underneath the fibre edge and lift it up and back, stretching it at the same time, to reveal the top edge circle line. This creates a short funnel neck of fibre standing vertically from the top edge circle line.

Step 9: Finishing layer one fibre layout

Continue to lay out the remaining layer one fibre all over the ball, infilling any thinner areas and creating an even thickness of fibre all over, including the funnel neck fibre at the top of the ball. Note that you only need to add fibre on the outside of the extended area, not the inside nearest the ball.

Step 10: Completing layers two and three fibre layout

Repeat the dunk and place method to add the next two 33g layers of fibre evenly to the ball, but keep the funnel neck area, especially the join/fold at the top edge circle line, slightly thinner. Pat regularly to check evenness, smooth the fibres down with soapy hands and add any extra fibre you feel necessary to thicken thin areas.

Step 11: Covering the fibre in plastic

Generously spray the fibre and wrap in plastic up to the top edge circle line. Fold back the funnel neck fibre over the plastic, ensuring that the plastic stays in the fold. The height of the funnel neck fibre (which isn't covered in plastic) should still measure at least 4cm (1.5in). For a bigger bowl rim, add more fibre now to extend it.

Step 12: Preparing to rub the fibre

Cover the exposed fibre with another piece of plastic. Stretch one pair of tights over the 28cm (11in) internal diameter rubbing bowl, place the ball inside and gently pull up the edges of the tights as high as they will go. Repeat with the second pair of tights, this time placing the ball inside to cover the area not covered by the first pair.

Step 13: Rubbing the fibre

Place the ball inside the bowl, pour on soapy water to ensure the whole ball and tights are soaked, and gently push the ball around the bowl in all directions, ensuring that the ball makes contact with the sides of the bowl but not pushing so hard that the fibres are moved out of place. Repeat the pushing/rubbing action for 400 pushes.

Step 14: Neatening the top edge

Remove the tights and plastic pieces and spray the ball all over. Lift up the rim fibre and insert your fingers at the fibre fold join on the inside next to the ball. With the other hand at the fibre join on the outside, rub the join to smooth it. Then neaten the fibre edge by fluffing it up, folding it inwards towards the *inside* and gently rubbing.

Step 15: Completing the rubbing

Replace the main plastic, fold back the rim fibre as in Step 11, cover the rim fibre with plastic and place the ball in tights. Repeat the push rub action for 400 pushes twice more, pushing more firmly each time. Remove the ball from the tights and plastic after each round to spray, rub and smooth the rim fibre join and fibre edge.

Step 16: Bouncing the ball

Place the ball in the tights and bounce it on your work surface 500 times. The easiest method is to hold the tights above the ball whilst bouncing. After 500 bounces, remove the tights/plastic to check/rub the opening edges as before. Repeat this process at least three more times, alternating ball placement in the tights each time.

Step 17: Removing the ball

The fibre around the ball should now feel much firmer, tighter and thicker. If not, replace the tights and complete a further round of 500 bounces or more until the fibre is feeling more solid and fully integrated with itself. Remove the tights and plastic, deflate the ball and remove it from the prefelt bowl shape.

Step 18: Checking the embellishments

Check the embellishments are well bonded on the inside. If there are still lots of loose elements, particularly the fabric, first give the inside a good soapy spray. Then reinsert the ball and put the ball/bowl back in the rubbing bowl. Pour on soapy water and rub the ball/bowl around directly with your hands for 400 rubs. Remove the ball.

Step 19: Throwing the bowl

Dunk the bowl completely in soapy water and gently squeeze. Gently pick it up and throw it on the work surface 50 times, spinning the bowl around on its sides as you throw and maintaining the rounded shape at all times. Then rub around the rim with your fingers to neaten the edge and slightly stretch it.

Step 20: Rubbing the embellishments inside

Spray the inside again and, with very soapy hands, rub the embellishments all over, avoiding moving your hands too much. Repeat Step 19 for another 50 throws, then wet and rub the inside again. Repeat throwing and rubbing for 300 throws in total, by which time the embellishments should be sinking into the felt and bonding well.

Step 21: Rubbing the embellishments outside

Turn the bowl right side out and, again with soapy hands, rub the embellishments directly to encourage further embedding. Check over the embellishments and trim anything which is loose, if preferred.

Step 22: Rolling the rim edge

Flatten the bowl and, with soapy hands, roll the rim edge towards the embellished side to neaten the edge and shape the rim and encourage it to stay in position. Repeat all around the edge. Then rinse the bowl under warm running water, or soak in bowls of warm water, squeezing gently until the water runs clear.

Step 23: Finishing the bowl

Remove excess water by rolling the bowl up in a dry towel. Reinsert the ball (I used the smaller green ball) and inflate as much as possible to stretch and smooth the bowl's surface and set the rounded shape. Roll the rim down. Deflate and remove the ball. Gently flatten the bowl's base on the work surface and leave to air dry.

SARI SILK HAT

We're combining two projects here: the Slouchy Hat from Chapter 3 for the structure, and the Sari Silk Bowl for the surface design and rim/brim. This hat version uses exactly the same weights and measurements as the Slouchy Hat (large purple felting ball, inflated to 80cm/31.5in circumference; 90g of carded wool fibre, in this case Finnwool; and the same target size of no less than 33cm × 28cm × 28cm/13in × 11in × 11in). However, we're shaping the felt differently and using all-sari silk materials as embellishment.

There is plenty of extra felt in the top of the hat to shape it how you would like. I pushed the top of the hat straight down, rather than angling it backwards as I did for the Slouchy Hat, and created two pleats/folds 4cm (1.5in) apart at the sides, 4cm (1.5in) from the brim fold to the first fold, then 4cm (1.5in) to the second fold. The best way to mould the shape as you would like is to place it on your head and experiment, and use pegs to hold the pleats as it dries.

Unlike the Sari Silk Bowl, the end size is crucial here and, depending on the fibre and materials you use, you might find that you have to overfelt the fibre to achieve a good bond with the materials, which might mean your hat ends up too small. It's interesting to note that the bowl, which started out with the same ball circumference size as the hat and a similar amount of fibre, ended up 5cm (2in) smaller in circumference than the hat by the end because I had to felt it more to ensure the embellishments were fully bonded. So this is definitely a project you should test first. For this hat I used Finnwool and

less embellishments, and found that I could keep the starting ball size the same as for the Slouchy Hat to still achieve the finished target hat opening circumference of 56cm (22in). If your test ends up too small, then just increase the starting ball size and target felting sizes accordingly.

Hat materials: Finnwool carded wool batt fibre and sari silk chunky yarn, blend fibres, ribbon yarn and fabric.

Sari silk embellishment layout on the ball.

Finnwool fibre layout complete, with 5–6cm (2in–2.25in) 'funnel neck' extension.

Hat at prefelt stage.

Shaping the hat whilst wearing.

SILK COWL PROJECT

For our final nuno felting project we are creating a cowl or infinity scarf using a complete layer of Margilan silk fabric, just 35g of Merino combed wool tops, and variegated bamboo tops as our surface embellishment. With this project I hope to show that you can felt on a ball with delicate Merino tops and create lightweight, drapey felt, not just the sturdier structural felt of our previous projects. And in fact because we are using so little fibre in this project, and because the nature of felting on a ball is quite hands-off initially in terms of the embellishment materials (which is ideal for nuno felting), this project felts like a dream.

There's always a challenge to be had, however, and the challenge with this project is in the layout. This is because in order to achieve a decent height with our cowl so that we can slouch it when wearing, we are doubling over the layout on the ball. The reason for this is all to do with working on a sphere. A cowl is basically a joined, circular 3D piece which, when laid flat, is a square or rectangle shape with straight sides. Although you can see how the continuous circle of fabric would be easy to achieve on a ball, what of course you don't get from working on a spherical shape is straight sides, instead they are curved inwards at the top and bottom. So to try and get the straightest edges possible we're only going to use the central area of the ball, from top edge line to base edge line, for our layout so that the curve at the sides isn't too great. This would be fine on its own but doesn't give us much height with our cowl. In order to achieve a decent height, we're therefore going to double the materials over to give us 40cm (16in) before felting, which leads to a finished felted height of around 28–33cm (11–13in), depending on the direction of our fibres and shrinkage technique.

The felting on a ball process is quite different for this project. We're going to lay out our materials in two halves, which I refer to as layer one and two, divided by a layer of plastic in between to stop them felting together. It's a bit fiddly, especially to get everything even at the fold, but the reward comes in the nature of everything felting very quickly and the fact that we can easily do lots of adjustment once we're at prefelt stage and have removed the ball. So it's not a difficult project to get a good result.

Materials

- Approximately 35g of Merino combed wool tops in your chosen colours, divided into two lengths each measuring approximately 105cm (41.5in) and weighing 17–18g
- I used extra-fine 19 micron Merino wool tops in the following combination:

Layout Element	Colour	Amount
Layer 1	Shocking pink	18g
Layer 2	Bright turquoise	17g

- 96.5cm × 43cm (38in × 17in) piece of Margilan silk fabric (I used variegated pink)
- Approximately 15g of silky embellishment tops (I used bamboo tops in variegated pinks) divided into two lengths each measuring approximately 105cm (41.5in) and weighing 7.5g

Equipment

- Large purple felting ball, inflated to 91.5cm (36in) circumference
- Inflating pump
- 25cm (10in) internal diameter round bowl or similar to prop up the ball
- Large bowl of any size to hold the washing-up liquid and warm water solution
- 32cm (12.5in) minimum internal diameter round or square bowl to push rub the ball within
- Two pairs of XXL (137–152cm/54–60in hips) tights/pantyhose, 20 denier (*see* Chapter 1 for preparation)
- Two 100cm × 30cm (40in × 12in) pieces of thin plastic
- Washing-up/dishwashing liquid
- Olive oil soap
- Spray bottle (containing washing-up liquid and warm water solution)
- Several large towels
- Several small/tea towels
- Scales
- Tape measure
- Large scissors
- Iron
- Ironing board

In terms of materials, although this will work with any kind of silk fabric that you know will felt well, I would recommend investing in some Margilan silk to try this with, certainly for the first time. It's so fine and felts so well and easily that it's a joy to felt and will make the longer layout time worthwhile. I've used hand-dyed Margilan silk, combined with extra-fine 19 micron Merino wool tops (but any Merino wool tops would be fine), in two colours. You can lay out the Merino tops in any way you like, either as wisps in a chevron or herringbone pattern or randomly. Alternatively you could use the stretched-out method I've used for a very quick and easy layout, or use a fine layer of a carded Merino batt or even a fine Merino prefelt. Just be aware that the stretched-out method when using tops (which are combed and not carded) has meant that directionally all my fibres are going around in line with the width of the cowl, so I've had more shrinkage in that direction (the width) as a result. The width is our key target measurement for when we stop felting – the height can be variable – so mine felted very quickly. When I've made similar cowls using a chevron layout the shrinkage was more even in both directions, so I had to focus more during fulling to reduce the width.

I've included variegated stripe bamboo tops for the surface embellishment, which I've also stretched out to use, creating lines going mainly along the width but not providing a full surface layer. If you prefer a complete layer then it would work better to lay the tops out in overlapping wisps. You could use any similar tops, such as viscose or silk, for a similar sheen effect.

This is quite a forgiving project in terms of making adjustments – once the ball has been removed we can stretch or reduce where we need to, in order to achieve straight edges and reduce the width to a good size (the height is less crucial). I've gone for a finished size of 30.5cm (12in) wide, but you can stop sooner if you would like a wider cowl. We can also roll the fabric/felt edges to create a rolled hem effect.

The finished cowl weighs approximately 50g and measures approximately 30.5cm wide × 33cm high (12in × 13in), or 61cm (24in) in circumference.

Step by Step

Step 1: Assembling your materials

Collect your wool and bamboo tops fibre and silk fabric together to create a pleasing colour palette. If using the stretched-out layout method for your wool/bamboo tops, to ensure you keep your fibre in a continuous piece measure/cut a 105cm (41.5in) length of tops then weigh it and peel away strips until you reach the desired weight.

Step 2: Preparing your wool fibre

Gently stretch out the first 17g/105cm (41.5in) length of wool tops fibre to create a fine and even rectangle of wispy fibre measuring approximately 100cm × 21cm (39.5in × 8.25in). Note that the length will reduce as you stretch the width. Repeat for the second length of wool tops fibre.

Step 3: Preparing your other materials/equipment

Repeat Step 2 to stretch out each 7.5g/105cm (41.5in) length of bamboo tops in a similar way. Carefully put all four fibre rectangle pieces aside. Cut off any selvedge from the silk fabric to remove thickness. Inflate the felting ball to 91.5cm (36in) in circumference and place on the propping-up ball with the base side up.

Step 4: Laying out the first silk fabric layer

Take the silk fabric and place it around the ball, lining up the long edge of the fabric with the base edge line of the ball and spraying lightly to secure. Overlap the two short ends of fabric where they meet. Note that the rest of the fabric (for the second, folded-over layer) will be hanging down.

Step 5: Adjusting the first silk fabric layer

Spray lightly and press the fabric onto the ball in the entire area between the base edge line and the top design line. Adjust the silk fabric as necessary to even out any creases or folds. Once adjusted, trim the overlap of the short edges to a minimum 1.5cm (0.5in) overlap.

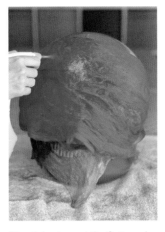

Step 6: Laying out the first wool fibre layer

Take the first long rectangle piece of wool fibre and place it on top of the silk, lining up the long edge of the fibre with the base edge line of the ball and the long edge of the silk. Spray and press down to secure. Overlap the two short ends of fibre and then remove/wisp the ends to reduce bulk and create an even thickness join.

Step 7: Creating the fibre overlap

Gather together the loose silk fabric for layer two at the top of the ball to keep it out of the way. Then create an overlap of the fibre at the main fold line by wisping up the edge of the fibre so that it extends beyond the top design line by at least 1cm (0.5in). Later, this will fold onto layer two to ensure there is no gap in fibre.

Step 8: Laying out the first bamboo fibre layer

Repeat Step 6 to add the first long rectangle piece of bamboo fibre on top of the wool layer. Adjust and wisp out the fibre to create as even a layer as possible. Then fluff out the fibre to just beyond the top design line edge in the same way as with the wool fibre in Step 7.

Step 9: Adding the first plastic layer

Add the first piece of plastic on top of the bamboo fibre layer, carefully lining up the long edge of the plastic with the top design line edge and overlapping the short ends of the plastic where they meet. The other long edge of the plastic should cover and extend beyond the base edge line of the ball and the other long edges of the layout.

Step 10: Laying out the second bamboo fibre layer

The layer one layout is now complete and we are repeating the layout in reverse for layer two. First fold over and wisp out the bamboo fibre overlap from layer one onto layer two. Then repeat Step 8, adding the second long rectangle piece of bamboo fibre on top between the top design line and base edge lines. Spray to secure.

Step 11: Laying out the second wool fibre layer

Next fold over the wool fibre overlap from layer one onto layer two. Then repeat Step 6 to add the second long rectangle piece of wool fibre on top between the top design line and base edge lines. Spray to secure.

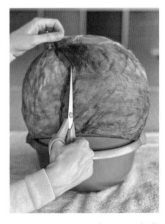

Step 12: Laying out the second silk fabric layer

Fold over the loose silk fabric onto the second wool layer, ensuring a close, neat fold along the top design line edge. Repeat Steps 4 and 5 to adjust and smooth out the fabric as necessary and trim the overlap of the short edges. Finally, trim any excess fabric along the two long edges. Spray and cover with the second piece of plastic.

Step 13: Preparing to rub the fibre

Stretch one pair of tights over the 32cm (12.5in) internal diameter rubbing bowl, place the ball inside and gently pull up the edges of the tights as high as they will go. Repeat with the second pair, this time placing the ball inside so that the area not covered by the first pair is covered. Pour on soapy water to soak the tights.

Step 14: Rubbing the fibre

Place the ball inside the bowl and gently push the ball around the bowl in all directions, ensuring that the ball makes contact with the sides of the bowl but not pushing so hard that the fibres are moved out of place. Repeat the pushing/rubbing action for 400 pushes.

Step 15: Neatening the edges

Peel each pair of tights away from the ball and back over the edges of the bowl, and place the ball on the propping-up bowl. Remove the top layer of plastic. Check both long edges of the silk/fibre and gently nudge any stray fibres back in line. Replace the plastic and tights and repeat Step 14 for 400 pushes twice more.

Step 16: Bouncing the ball

Place the ball in the tights and bounce it on your work surface 500 times. The easiest method is to hold the tights above the ball whilst bouncing. After 500 bounces, remove the tights/plastic to check the edges are still straight. Repeat this process once more, alternating ball placement in the tights each time, making 1,000 bounces.

Step 17: Removing the ball

Remove the tights and plastic and deflate the ball slightly, enough to enable you to peel up one edge of the cowl and check that the fibre has bonded to the silk, using a gentle pinch. If not, reinflate the ball, soak the fibre and continue bouncing for another 500 to 1,000 bounces. If it has bonded, fully deflate and remove the ball.

Step 18: Smoothing the fold

Carefully peel apart the two layers of the cowl and remove the inside plastic piece. Turn the cowl silk side out. Work along the fibre fold, gently stretching it to smooth out any folds in the silk fabric. Turn the cowl bamboo side out and gently wisp and smooth any folds in the fibre before rubbing flat along the fold line with a soapy hand.

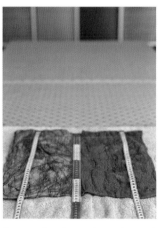

Step 19: Starting to shape the cowl

Lay the cowl flat and gently stretch the middle area to start squaring up the sides. The approximate flat width measurements at this stage are 38cm (15in) across the middle and 41cm (16in) across the top and bottom edges. The height is 38cm (15in). The next few steps will continue to even up the shape and shrink the cowl.

Step 20: Throwing the cowl

Soak the cowl in warm soapy water. With the cowl still fibre side out, pick it up in its circular shape and gently throw it on the work surface 200 times, spinning the cowl around as you throw and maintaining the circular shape at all times. The purpose is to gently encourage the felt to shrink and adhere fully to the fabric.

Step 21: Neatening the open edges

Flatten the cowl, with the fibre side still up, and neaten the open edges by trimming any excess silk fabric or fibres. Then to create neat, slightly rolled edges, spray and roll the edges inwards towards the fibre with a soapy hand. Repeat all along both edges. Continue to regularly roll the edges in this way until the cowl is finished.

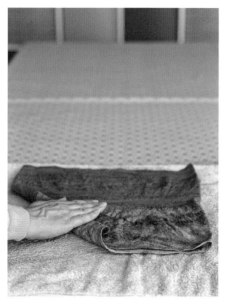

Step 22: Straightening the sides

To finish squaring up the shape, roll each of the slightly flared/curved side corners inwards towards the fibre for 20 rolls (80 in total). Then lift up the cowl, change the fold position and repeat. This will help to shrink the flared/curved areas at the top and bottom of each side to become straighter. Repeat as necessary.

Step 23: Stretching the sides

Alternate Step 22 (rolling the corners inwards to reduce them) with stretching the middle area of the sides to expand them. Put your hands or arms inside the circle of fabric and gently stretch it. Alternating the Step 22 rolling and Step 23 stretching will encourage the sides to straighten.

Step 24: Shrinking the cowl

If the cowl still needs to shrink further (*see* Step 25 for the desired end size), to achieve general shrinkage all over roll it up on itself from each of the four sides/edges and roll for 20 rolls. If only the width needs reducing, just roll from the two side edges. If only the height needs reducing, just roll from the two open edges.

Step 25: Completing the fulling

Stop the straightening, edge rolling and shrinking actions when the cowl has reached a size of no less than 32.5cm (12.75in) wide. Try it over your head during the previous steps to check the fit and stop earlier than this if you would prefer a wider fit. The height can vary and is likely to be between 28cm–35.5cm (11in–14in).

Step 26: Finishing the cowl

Rinse or soak the cowl in warm water, squeezing gently until the water runs clear. Remove excess water by rolling it up in a dry towel, then reshape using any of the previous techniques to straighten it. Note that the width is likely to have shrunk to 30.5cm (12in). Leave to air dry. Once dry, steam iron to smooth the surface.

GREEN SILK COWL

Here's an alternative cowl with a simpler layout because it doesn't include a top embellishment layer. Instead I've used a Merino blend with tussah silk, so the embellishment is included within the fibre. As this was a stripey-effect tops blend I again used the stretched-out layout method to try and retain a sense of the stripes.

All the other measurements and instructions are the same as the main project, but the finished cowl weighs just 40g without the embellishment layer. However, it is still structurally sound and shows what a good job the Margilan silk does in adding to the strength of a piece when combined with a wool layer.

Green Margilan silk fabric and variegated Merino and tussah silk blend tops.

One of the two stretched-out wool fibre rectangles prepared for layout.

The first layer of silk fabric and wool fibre laid out on the ball.

Complete silk fabric and wool fibre layout on the ball prior to felting.

RECTANGULAR SILK VASE

For the final nuno felting variation, I wanted to show that you don't just have to use Margilan for delicate projects and with fine Merino wool, you can use it within sturdier structural projects too, and with coarser fibre. You also don't have to use it in a complete piece. So for this project I've created a studier vase from three colours of Finnwool fibre and used different colours of hand-dyed Margilan silk in smaller pieces to create a patchwork effect, which also offers some interesting colour blending. By laying the silk pieces in mostly vertical strips versus the fibre in horizontal bands, this achieves multiple colour combinations as the same piece of silk will look different in different areas depending on which colour of fibre is behind it. The fact that the Margilan is so fine works brilliantly for this.

Because it felts so well, Margilan silk is also great at trapping other materials underneath it, to create raised areas. I've used prefelt offcuts from previous projects to create simple leaf shapes, which I've placed between the silk and the wool fibre. The silk is so fine that you can see the prefelt colours and patterns coming through, which adds extra surface interest, as well as dimension.

Structure-wise, I folded over the top edge once I'd removed the ball and then continued to throw, rub and shape the vase with the turned-over edge in position as the bowl completed shrinking. I kept the edge turned over at all times, including during rinsing and towel drying, which helped to set it in place.

I also wanted to demonstrate that you can create a more straight-edged shape from felting on a ball, not just rounded. After removing the ball from the rounded prefelt shape, I used

a couple of boxes (first plastic and then a smaller cardboard box) during throwing and shaping to encourage and develop the finished rectangular shape. I left the final box inside as a finishing forma until the felt had dried.

Finnwool carded wool batt fibre in three colours (30g × 3 layers), yarn-embellished prefelt offcuts and a variety of hand-dyed strips of Margilan silk fabric.

Vertical layout of Margilan silk strips and prefelt leaf shapes on the medium green felting ball, inflated to 76cm (30in).

Finnwool fibre layout on the ball in horizontal stripes of yellow, green and turquoise for layers one and two, and solid turquoise for layer three.

Repurposing a cardboard box as a finishing forma to create the rectangular vase shape.

CHAPTER 6

DEVELOPING YOUR OWN PROJECTS

Hopefully by this stage in the book you've had a chance to try out some of the projects and adapt them to your own preferences about size, colour and type of fibre. You might also be starting to think about developing your own projects entirely, and wondering how to translate your ideas into successful designs. So this chapter aims to give you some pointers about developing your work to a theme, and how to work towards producing wet felted pieces which reflect your own creativity.

As an example, I'm going to share my approach to creating a new decorative wet felted piece in a theme which I find inspiring, to show you how I arrived at the end design. This isn't a step-by-step project, as I'm sure by now you've mastered the process for felting on a ball, attaching extra structural elements and using different surface design materials. My aim is to give you some further inspiration to change the felted surface more (either raising it or working into it, to become more 3D), which you can combine with any of the other techniques in this book, reflecting whatever subject you're passionate about.

CREATING FELT SAMPLES

I find that the most difficult stage of a new project is getting started, when you're pulling ideas together and not quite sure what you're aiming for or how to get there. My main advice, in addition to collecting design inspiration in the form of photographs/images and perhaps sketching out your ideas, is to make samples. Samples are a brilliant means not only of testing out your materials and techniques but also just getting you started. I often find inspiration from the materials themselves, so my starting point is usually pulling together all the different materials in a particular colourway that I have in mind, and then making samples with them. It definitely helps you to work out what you do and don't like, and gets you a step nearer to creating the final piece that's in your head. It also gets you into your project and helps ignite your interest and a bit of excitement for moving it forward.

Sampling requires a particular mindset, because of course we all want to just get on and make things straight away and for them to turn out perfect. But you learn so much from making samples first, with less pressure and expectations about the results, and for an important project it will really help you to work out what would work best so that you are not disappointed and wasting time and materials. So it always pays off and you will learn something from every sample, whether it's just how two colours have mixed together, whether an unknown piece of fabric or yarn will felt in or whether you've got the right starting size for the felting ball for a particular sized result.

And what can you do with those samples afterwards? Interesting flat samples could be put into a sample book, or sewn together to make a bigger art piece. You could cut up samples into smaller pieces to repurpose as raised areas in your main project – I'll be showing this technique within this chapter. And your samples don't have to be flat pieces. Creating small bowls/vessels is a great way to make samples and test out different materials, as you don't need to invest a lot of time or materials and you can easily scale up for a bigger version. You could pick a small-size bowl and create several samples using different wool fibres, materials or techniques, which would then give you a collection to display. There are always ways to use your samples so they aren't wasted, and you can still end up with a substantial item at the end.

JURASSIC BASKET PROJECT

I live at the start of the Jurassic Coast World Heritage Site in Devon, UK, not far from famous seaside locations such as Lyme Regis in Dorset where many Jurassic-era fossils have been found, in particular ammonites. So the whole subject of the coastline, beach, seashells and fossils is one which particularly interests me. My project idea was to create some sort of vessel or basket shape reflecting this theme and incorporating items such as locally found driftwood.

I've outlined below the main steps I took to create the finished basket design, highlighting the materials and techniques I incorporated.

STAGE 1: PULLING TOGETHER IDEAS AND MATERIALS

I started off by collecting photographs and images of ammonites, with the aim of incorporating a spiral ammonite design using a cutaway resist technique. From these initial images I drew a simple ammonite shape and created a stencil from this using 1mm thick foam.

Next I pulled together lots of different materials which I felt reflected the colours of polished ammonite fossils, in a distinct blue and copper colourway with some sheen. These included: variegated Finnwool carded wool batt fibre; Margilan silk fabric; sequined fabric; silk, viscose and bamboo tops; silk hankies; hand-spun chunky wool yarns; and Teeswater curly wool locks.

Carded wool fibre and embellishment materials used in the final basket.

Initial ammonite shape drawn on paper and foam resist created from it.

STAGE 2: CREATING SAMPLES

I created two flat, rectangular samples to test out the materials, colours and techniques. I laid out the fibre for each in two thick main layers, as all the techniques involved adding elements in between the two layers.

The 'Cracked Earth' or 'Cracked Mud' Technique

This involves cutting a design into the top layer of the felt, revealing another colour underneath. It uses a stencil-like resist within fibre layers, which creates channels within the felt where the layers aren't able to felt together because the resist has stopped them from bonding. Once the main fibre is fully bonded, usually at some point during the fulling process, you then cut into the layers from the outside, and into and along the channels, and remove the resist, which recreates the stencil design in cut lines in the felt. The design ideally needs to have lines which all join together, which when cut resemble cracked earth or similar. You just need to ensure that the outer layer of fibre and the layer which is revealed when you cut into the top layer are different colours, to really make the cut design stand out. Cutting the lines during the fulling stage enables you to give the cut lines a rub/shape and continue fulling, which ideally makes them look less like raw cut edges by the end. You'll see that I tried this technique on both sample pieces using a small foam resist representing three ammonite segments together.

The Cutaway Resist Technique

This also involves using resist shapes within the layers of fibre, but more separate, discrete shapes which don't need to be joined up. Again, at some point during fulling, you cut into the top layers of the felt to remove the resists and reveal what's underneath. You could cut away the whole shape from the front of the felt or just cut the shape open and peel back the felt like a flap. This also works really well if what's underneath the top layer of felt looks strikingly different colour or texture-wise. I tried this technique out on both samples, using single resist pieces to represent ammonite segment shapes, with different colours and/or fabric as the underneath layers. I used 5mm foam resists but any thickness would work.

Creating Raised Elements

Rather than using a resist within the layers and cutting into the felt to reduce it, you could do the opposite and raise up the surface of the felt by adding pieces of prefelt or felt. In my second sample I added pieces of felt within the two main layers of fibre (again to represent single ammonite segments), so they were well embedded, but you could add them on top of the final layer of fibre with just a little extra fibre or some embellishment fibres or fabric on top to keep them in place, as I did in the finished basket. The raised pieces can then be left as they are, or you could carve into them to reveal a portion of them, or cut around the edge of them as I did in the sample.

Creating Flap Layers

Another resist technique which you would set in place within the layers of the fibre during layout is to create attached, extra flaps of felt, which can then be cut into shapes and manipulated during the fulling stage. In my second sample I shaped a piece of thin plastic and placed it on top of part of the first layer towards one edge, with pieces of silk hankies above and below it to add interest to the flap layers once revealed. I then put the second main fibre layer on top. The plastic stopped the two areas from felting so that, once finished and I had removed the plastic, I had a large flap I could fold onto the front of the sample and cut into.

The completed flap layer on the second sample, showing the silk hankies embellishment on both the folded-down flap and the revealed area that was behind it. The silk hankies used are shown at the top.

The first sample made using the cracked earth and cutaway resist techniques, along with a chunky hand-spun yarn laid in a spiral underneath Margilan silk and viscose fibres (the chunky yarn twists resemble ammonite segments).

The initial layout of the second sample, with the cracked earth and cutaway resists on top of the first main layer of wool fibre, along with felt pieces to create raised elements. Note the Margilan silk and sequin fabrics under the resists, and the silk hankies at the bottom before thin plastic was laid on top to create a flap layer.

The finished layout for the second sample, with the second main layer of carded wool fibre on top of the resists, and various embellishment materials laid on top of the second layer of fibre (Margilan silk pieces, chunky hand-spun yarn underneath the silk, viscose, bamboo and silk tops and curly wool locks).

The second sample during the fulling stage, just before cutting into the top layer of felt to reveal the resists. Note the prominent bumps in the surface of the felt covering the resists, and how the red-brown silk fabric has tightened around the chunky hand-spun yarn spiral to create a raised shape.

The completed second sample after cutting the top layer to reveal the resists and raised elements underneath, along with some of the embellishment materials used. Note the two different types of foam resist shape used.

It's worth noting that you can make flat felt using the felting on a ball technique, which is how I made the two samples, although I could, of course, have made them as 3D samples on the ball. The trick is to use bubble wrap and plastic to hold the flat felt in place before wrapping it around the ball. Here's how I did it:

- I laid out the fibre and embellishments for each sample on bubble wrap, sandwiching them between layers to create a package. I then placed a large sheet of thin plastic over the rubbing bowl, and laid the flat fibre package on top. I pushed the ball down on top of the package and folded the edges of the package around the ball, before wrapping the plastic around to keep the bubble wrap package in place. I placed everything in two pairs of tights as usual and followed the usual felting process for each sample

(3 × 400 rounds of push rubs and 2 × 500 rounds of bounces – I found that two rounds were sufficient as there was a lot less fibre in the samples than would normally be used on the ball, but you could do more rounds if necessary. I unwrapped and checked/adjusted the fibre after each round as usual).

- Once I was happy that the fibre had become a stable prefelt, I removed the tights, plastic and bubble wrap and completed 300 throws on the table, by which point the felt was clearly shrinking and becoming firmer. I completed any cutting out of resists and cutting into the felt at this point, before rubbing the cut edges to firm them. I then completed 200 more throws whilst continuing to rub the cut edges, rub around the raised elements to accentuate them and stretch the large layer/flap. I rinsed the pieces and left them to air dry.

Using a rubbing bowl and large piece of thin plastic to help wrap the felt sample piece around the ball, prior to felting.

The flat sample piece sandwiched in bubble wrap and held in place around the ball by the large plastic piece wrapped around it.

STAGE 3: FELTING THE MAIN PROJECT

Creating the samples was an invaluable stage as it helped me to refine some of the aspects (colours, materials and techniques) and make decisions about what I did or didn't want to take forward to the final project piece. Here are some brief conclusions I drew from the samples, along with how I translated those to the main basket project (much of which were simply down to my personal preference and the elements I felt best supported the ammonite and coastal theme):

- Colour-wise, I wanted to reduce the amount of red brown and brighter green embellishment materials to focus on blues, darker browns and copper shades.
- I liked the silky sheen brought by the Margilan silk pieces, all the tops fibres (viscose, bamboo and silk) and the silk hankies so incorporated a lot of this on the surface of the finished basket.
- I liked the segment-like effect of the chunky hand-spun twisted yarn under the Margilan silk, but wanted to move away from the bright green colour so chose a paler colour to use instead.
- With the cracked earth technique, if the segments in between the lines of the resist are very small, the fibres in that segment sometimes don't bond well and the whole segment pulls away completely. So in the finished basket I avoided using very small segments in the centre of the ammonite spiral and instead used a cutaway centre with a sequined fabric behind.
- One of the trickiest aspects with the cracked earth technique is finding the resist from the outside, as the thin foam within the layers is hard to locate. So in the final basket layout I measured various points and noted the positioning of other elements so that I would be able to find the resist more easily.
- I liked the look of the blue sequined fabric when cut away, but decided that it would look more effective if used sparingly, hence I only used it in the centre of the ammonite spiral.
- I preferred the look of the raised segments under Margilan silk (rather than other fibres) as the silk really hugs the outline of the segments well. I reused part of the folded layer in the second sample to cut out segments to use under the surface of the silk.

To create the basket, I followed the usual felting on a ball process of working inside out to lay out the embellishments and wool fibre, and the usual number of rounds of the push rub, bouncing and throwing stages. Here are some of the key points to note, including a few differences:

- I inflated the purple felting ball to 91.5cm (36in) in circumference and used 150g of variegated blue and brown Finnwool carded wool batt fibre.
- To ensure the basket would still be thick enough to maintain a good sturdy structure after cutting away the ammonite resist, I divided the carded wool fibre into four layers rather than the usual three, so that the resist would have two layers of fibre both above and below it. I used approximately 37g of fibre per layer, in a mix of the blue and brown colours for the first three layers, and blue for the final (inside) layer.
- I wanted to incorporate a piece of driftwood as a handle so I raised up the handle layout at the sides of the basket to follow the A and C segments at the top of the basket.
- The initial embellishment fibre layout on the ball consisted of the following: tops fibres, silk hankies, Margilan silk fabric strips, wool yarns, curly wool locks and, behind the silk strips, ammonite segment pieces made from the sample felt. I then added two layers of fibre, before placing the ammonite resist on top, covered by a central piece of blue sequined fabric and a piece of blue Margilan silk fabric. I also placed silk hankies either side of a piece of plastic along both front and back top edges to create flap layers. I completed the layout with two further layers of wool fibre.
- After following the usual felting process and removing the ball, I soaked the inside of the basket and did a combination of rubbing the inside and gentle throwing for 300 throws. At that point I turned the basket right side out and carefully cut into the ammonite shape and removed the resist. I also cut into the flap layers front and back, creating two long, thin strips each side. Finally I cut a hole in each handle. I rubbed all the cut edges with soapy hands before completing a further 200 throws along with stretching/shaping the inside of the basket, rinsing and towel drying.
- Before leaving the basket to dry, I reshaped it inside and twisted the thin hanging strips into pleasing shapes. Once dry, I stitched them in place with embroidery thread, hiding the stitches within the felt, and pushed the driftwood handle through the holes to finish.

Temporary placement of the ammonite resist template during initial layout of the embellishment fibres.

Actual placement of the ammonite resist template after laying out the first two layers of fibre.

The finished ammonite design using the cracked earth technique with a central cutaway revealing sequined fabric.

Placement of the ammonite segment felt pieces behind Margilan silk fabric during initial embellishment layout, to create raised elements.

The finished raised ammonite segments covered by Margilan silk fabric and viscose fibres.

Shaped plastic resist inserted between fibre layers two and three, and covered by silk hankies each side, to create a fold-down flap of felt.

The finished flap layer of silk-covered felt at the front of the basket, cut into thin strips, twisted and secured with a few stitches.

Finished smaller flap layer at the back of the basket, also cut into thin strips, twisted and hand-sewn in place.

Final layer of wool fibre on the ball, showing the extended layout of the two handles.

One of the finished handles showing the hole in the middle with the driftwood handle inserted through.

CHAPTER 7

FINISHING YOUR FELT

nce we've made our felted items and they've dried, there are still some steps we might want to take to finish them off. That may be to install some sort of closure, like a zip or clasp on a bag, or to neaten the surface of the felt by trimming loose hairs or fibres. So here are some ideas for finishing your felt, starting with some general tips to tweak the shape and surface before covering specific techniques for installing closures. I've also included some tips on caring for your felt. All of these will add and maintain that final polish and professional finish to the felt which you've worked so hard to create.

TRIMMING

Wool fibre is hairy, so however smooth your finished felt ends up, it will always have a halo of fluffiness on the surface. Felt made from coarser fibres might well have identifiable thicker hairs poking up too, and embellishment materials such as mohair yarns can add a full hairy layer on top of the felt. So if you'd prefer a smoother result, don't be afraid to trim the fibres. I usually do this with large scissors, but you could also use a safety razor or a pilling tool (hand or battery-operated). You don't want to accidentally cut the felt, but a close trim or shave just eliminates the additional hairiness to give your felt a cleaner surface.

One way of reducing hairiness is to add non-wool embellishment materials to your surface layout. The finer, silkier embellishment fibres, such as silk hankies, silk tops and viscose/bamboo tops, seem to work best for this as they provide a fine layer all over which appears to reduce the wool fibre's ability to get through to the outside.

You might also want to trim your embellishment materials, perhaps if there is an element which hasn't felted in well or there is a random end poking out. I like to check for anything obvious and give it a snip at prefelt stage once I've removed the ball, on the basis that any changes won't be obvious after the fibre movement of the subsequent fulling stage, but you might also spot things once the felt has dried.

Trimming the edges of the floral basket with large scissors.

Removing wool fibres and pilling with a pilling tool.

IRONING

As a general rule, steam ironing finished felt is a really effective way to add a bit of polish to the surface because it smooths down all the fibres beautifully. Obviously you don't want to flatten something you've created to be deliberately 3D, but if you stuff the item with a towel and avoid applying too much pressure you should be able to smooth the surface rather than squash the shape. So if you do just one thing to finish off your felt, I would recommend ironing.

If your felt has ended up very crinkled, an iron will help to smooth out some of the wrinkles, although is unlikely to completely make them disappear as by this point they will have become an intrinsic part of the structure of the felt. The best ways to create a smooth result are to smooth wrinkles during fulling and stretch them out as the piece dries using a finishing forma.

Steam ironing is also useful if you need to reshape the felt slightly, perhaps to smooth out a lump or to stretch an uneven edge. The steam puts moisture and heat back into the felt, which gives you a quick opportunity to do some minor shaping, stretching or rubbing.

Obviously the main thing you have to be careful of with ironing is not to accidentally melt anything, such as synthetic sparkly fibres you might have used as part of your surface design (which will melt) or bubble wrap you might have put inside to help shape your item. You can also damage items like leather-backed magnetic clasps if the iron gets too close. So always iron before you install any closures or other additions.

Ironing the backpack to smooth the surface fibres.

REWETTING

When you've just finished a piece, it's not always easy to tell how thick and well felted it really is as the water is adding extra weight and volume. Sometimes it's not until it's dry that you can really tell. So if the dried felt still feels a little thin or the piece isn't holding its shape or structure well, then you could always try rewetting it and fulling it further to shrink and thicken it a little bit more. Soak the felt in very warm soapy water and give it 100–300 additional throws/rubs/scrunches, and you'll find that will work wonders.

Soaking the coiled rope vessel in warm soapy water before re-fulling.

PICKING AWAY

Carded wool fibre in particular often contains additional specks of organic matter, especially tiny pieces of straw. I tend not to worry too much about picking those out during the initial fibre preparation and layout, as often they are hidden or have disappeared by the time they have been through the full felting and rinsing process. But if any pieces remain and are obvious by the end, just treat them as you would a splinter in your finger and pick them out with the point of a needle.

HAND-SEWING A ZIP INTO AN OPENING

Here is a very simple hand-sewing method to install a zip into an opening for a cushion (or bag). To start with, I've found that it makes it easier to install if you have a much larger zip than you need, as then you can move the zip pull right out of the way for clearer sewing access. So I tend to have a stock of longer 40.5cm (16in) zips and cut them down to fit any project. Bear in mind that the zip needs to be open during all of the sewing, although there are times when we will close it to check the fit. I also turned the cushion right side out several times during sewing to check the fit and look from the outside.

You will need a standard 40.5cm (16in) zip, matching sewing thread, a sewing needle, scissors and pins. We are not using an invisible zip but it is mostly hidden on the outside when finished. We will also be sewing into the thickness of the felt, rather than going right through to the other side with our stitches, so that there are no stitches visible on the outside. I only did one row of stitches as the zip is not going to be subject to much wear once the cushion pad is inside, but you could go back over the stitching for a second pass (as I did for the Star Bag Project in Chapter 5).

Step 1: Pinning the first side

Remove the cushion pad and turn the cushion inside out. Unzip the zip. Starting at the end without the zip pull (the base end), pin one side of the zip to one edge of the felt opening, as shown, with the zip teeth edge at least 3mm from the edge of the felt. The plastic zip stopper should be at least 1cm from the start of the opening.

Step 2: Sewing the first side

Sew a parallel line of stitches along the zip, approximately 8mm from the zip teeth edge, removing the pins as you sew. Use a simple running stitch, but make each stitch in one motion (as you do when pinning) so that you are just sewing into the felt and out again with the needle before pulling the thread out.

Step 3: Sewing the second side

Close the zip to check it works, then reopen it and repeat Steps 1 and 2 to pin and sew the second side in the same way. Ensure that the base ends (the ends without the zip pull when the zip is open) are aligned when you start pinning. Before sewing too far along the edge, just check that you can still move the zip pull along.

Step 4: Securing the zip end

Move the zip pull into the cushion opening and cut off the excess zip approximately 4cm (1.5in) from the end of the opening. To ensure the zip pull cannot come off the end, oversew the zip teeth approximately 2.5cm (1in) from the end of the opening, sewing many times over the zip teeth and into the felt each time to secure it.

INVISIBLE CLASP STITCHING METHOD

When making items like bags and purses, where you see both the inside and outside of the item, attaching sew-on closure clasps neatly can be a bit of a headache when you don't have a lining to hide the stitches behind or if the clasp is on the inside and the stitches would therefore be obvious on the outside of the bag. So I've developed a method of hand-sewing a clasp to a bag which is largely invisible on the other side.

There are lots of different types of clasp you might use on a bag, but this is particularly useful for the type of leather-backed magnetic clasp closure I've used in the Dartmoor Basket Bag Project in Chapter 4. The clasp already comes with sewing holes, and the basic premise is that we are back-stitching through each hole for strength and hiding the stitches within the thickness of the felt.

Here's an example of the process, for which you'll need a clasp, a sewing needle, scissors and embroidery or sewing thread to match the clasp. For the purposes of this example, the *inside* refers to where the clasp is positioned and the *outside* refers to the other side of the felt. The pin is used as a marker. When you have completed Step 10, repeat Steps 4 to 10, moving along one hole each round, until you have sewn the whole clasp.

Step 1: Sew a couple of stitches on the inside underneath where the clasp will go, to hide and secure the thread knot.

Step 2: Push the needle up through the first clasp hole (1), pull the thread through and position the clasp over the knot.

Step 3: Push the needle down through the next hole along (2) to complete the first stitch inside and pull right through to the outside.

Step 4: Push a pin down through the next hole along (3) right through to the outside.

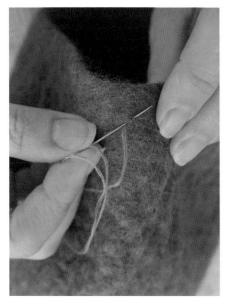

Step 5: On the outside, angle the needle and make a stitch into the felt from exactly where the thread exits the felt to exactly where the pin exits the felt.

Step 6: Pull the thread through to its new exit position on the outside to hide the stitch within the thickness of the felt and remove the pin.

Step 7: Make a stitch straight back into the felt from exactly where the thread now exits the felt, which should match up with hole (3).

Step 8: Pull the needle and thread through hole (3) on the inside.

Step 9: Note the thread disappearing on the outside.

Step 10: Push the needle down through hole (2) to complete the second stitch inside and pull right through to the outside.

Step 11: Once you have completed the final stitch through the clasp, and the needle and thread are on the outside, simply tie a knot in the thread close to the exit hole. Put the needle back through the hole on the outside, at an angle so that it emerges on the inside just under the very edge of the clasp. Pull the needle and knot through so that the knot is hidden within the felt and snip the excess thread to finish.

INSTALLING A TURN-LOCK CLASP

A great way of securing a bag with a flap, or any design where you have one piece of fabric folding over another to close the inside, is to install a turn or twist-lock clasp. They are easy to install and give a neat professional finish, with the bonus of not requiring any sewing! There are lots of different styles and shapes available, but the basic concept is that it is a two-part clasp: the upper part (which itself has separate front and back parts) frames a hole in the upper piece of fabric (in our case, the flap); and the lower part adds a protruding part to the lower fabric (in our case, the front of the bag). When you put the framed hole over the protruding part (in our case, put the flap down over the front of the bag), the top of the lower part turns or twists to secure the hole (flap) in place.

Here's an example of the process for attaching a turn-lock clasp to the backpack to secure the flap to the front pocket, for which you'll need a clasp, pen or pencil, scissors, textile glue (optional), screwdriver, seam ripper (optional), pins and ruler or tape measure. Key points to bear in mind are:

- Ensure the flap is pulled down tight over the front edge of the backpack and everything looks central before you start measuring and marking.
- Avoid cutting the hole too big initially, aim instead to stretch the felt hole around the framed hole in the clasp to make it fit. The same goes for the prong holes, aim to make the slits smaller initially and then force the prongs through to fit.

- You don't have to use glue, I just prefer to for extra security. Equally you don't need to use a seam ripper to make the prong holes, use scissors if preferred.

See also the Flap Bag variation project for a tuck lock clasp which is similar to install but doesn't involve cutting a hole in the flap.

Metal turn-lock clasp components and slider rings to install the strap.

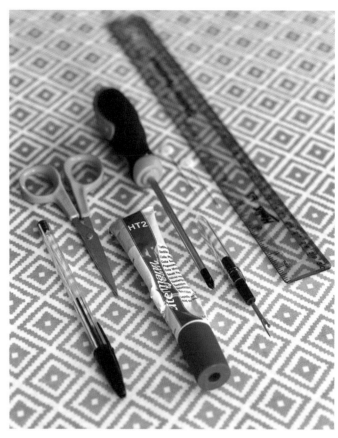

Equipment needed to install the turn-lock clasp.

Step 1: Position the smooth-sided front metal part with the hole on top of the flap, ensuring that it meets the front of the inside pocket when the flap is down. Draw around the inside of the hole.

Step 2: Carefully cut around the hole, cutting through the full thickness of the flap. Trim the hole on the reverse side also to neaten the edge. Be conservative in your trimming at this stage to avoid making the hole too big.

Step 3: Place the smooth-sided front metal part on top of the hole and, from the reverse, stretch the felt to fit around the hole frame. The hole also needs to fit around the screw holes. Carefully trim further as necessary.

Step 4: Add glue to the reverse of the smooth-sided front metal part and place it down onto the hole on the front of the flap. Turn the flap/backpack over and press against the work surface to secure.

Step 5: Ensure the felt hole is still around the inner hole frame and that the screw holes are fully accessible. Trim further as necessary. Then glue the reverse of the textured back metal part and place it on top of the installed clasp.

Step 6: Place the two screws into the screw holes and tighten with a screwdriver to secure. From the front of the flap, if the clasp/hole has rotated slightly you can gently rotate it back. Trim any fibres caught in the hole between the two parts.

Step 7: With the flap folded down over the front of the backpack, use two pins to mark the inside edges of the clasp hole. Carefully lift up the flap, keeping the pins in place. Check they are central to the pocket/backpack; repeat/adjust as necessary.

Step 8: Cut small (3mm) slits in the front pocket to match the pin marks, using either a seam ripper or scissors. Don't remove the pins until you have installed the prongs otherwise the slits become difficult to see. Push the prongs through the slits.

Step 9: Remove the pins and add the metal washer to the prongs on the reverse of the front pocket. Separately fold the prongs back onto the washer as firmly as you can. If preferred, glue or sew a label or piece of felt on top to cover the prongs.

CARING FOR YOUR FELT

Although felt is quite hardy, it is still fabric and, particularly for items subject to heavy usage (like a bag), it may start to show signs of wear. So here are some tips for keeping your felt looking its best.

Storage

For decorative items, such as a felt bowl or vase, avoid displaying it in direct sunlight as the colours will fade. For items like a bag, when not in use ideally keep your bag empty or filled with tissue paper or bubble wrap to help keep its shape. Store it somewhere it won't get squashed against other things, either hanging from its handles/strap or standing on its base. If it does get squashed, its structural memory should enable you to just shape it back into position, but if that isn't enough then a gentle steam iron and reshaping it with your hands will work wonders to smooth the surface and revive the shape.

Cleaning

Felt is made of 100 per cent wool, so if it gets dirty just treat it as you would an item of wool clothing. Spot cleaning for dirty marks is probably the best option, using a gentle wool detergent. If your item needs a proper wash to clean it, then a gentle handwash in a wool detergent should be absolutely fine, just avoid too much agitation as resoaking, rubbing and rinsing are of course all techniques we've used to shrink our felt. Avoid using either a washing machine or tumble dryer as then you will have no control over the continued fulling process. If you have sewn on any parts such as a leather-backed magnetic clasp, it would be worth removing that first as it is likely to be damaged by washing. The all-metal clasps should be fine.

Once you have rinsed out the detergent, reshape the item and leave it to air dry (on a towel). Once dry, give it a gentle steam iron to help reshape it and smooth the surface fibres.

Usage

Felt is water-resistant to an extent so will withstand being out in light rain. If an item like a bag gets quite wet, just reshape it and leave it to air dry as soon as possible.

Just like under the arms of a wool jumper, felt will start to pill (form small balls of fluff on its surface) if it continually rubs against another surface, such as a bag against your body. If this happens, simply pull or snip off the fluff, or use a pilling tool to remove it. Again, a gentle steam iron will help to smooth all the surface fibres.

Finished felt may also need protecting against less considerate members of your household (although offcuts make good cat toys)!

CHAPTER 8

TEMPLATES AND TABLES

STAR BAG PROJECT

Star Template
(cut 2 from sequined fabric)

Star Bag Project (Chapter 5): Star Template

Scale: actual size

DARTMOOR BASKET BAG PROJECT

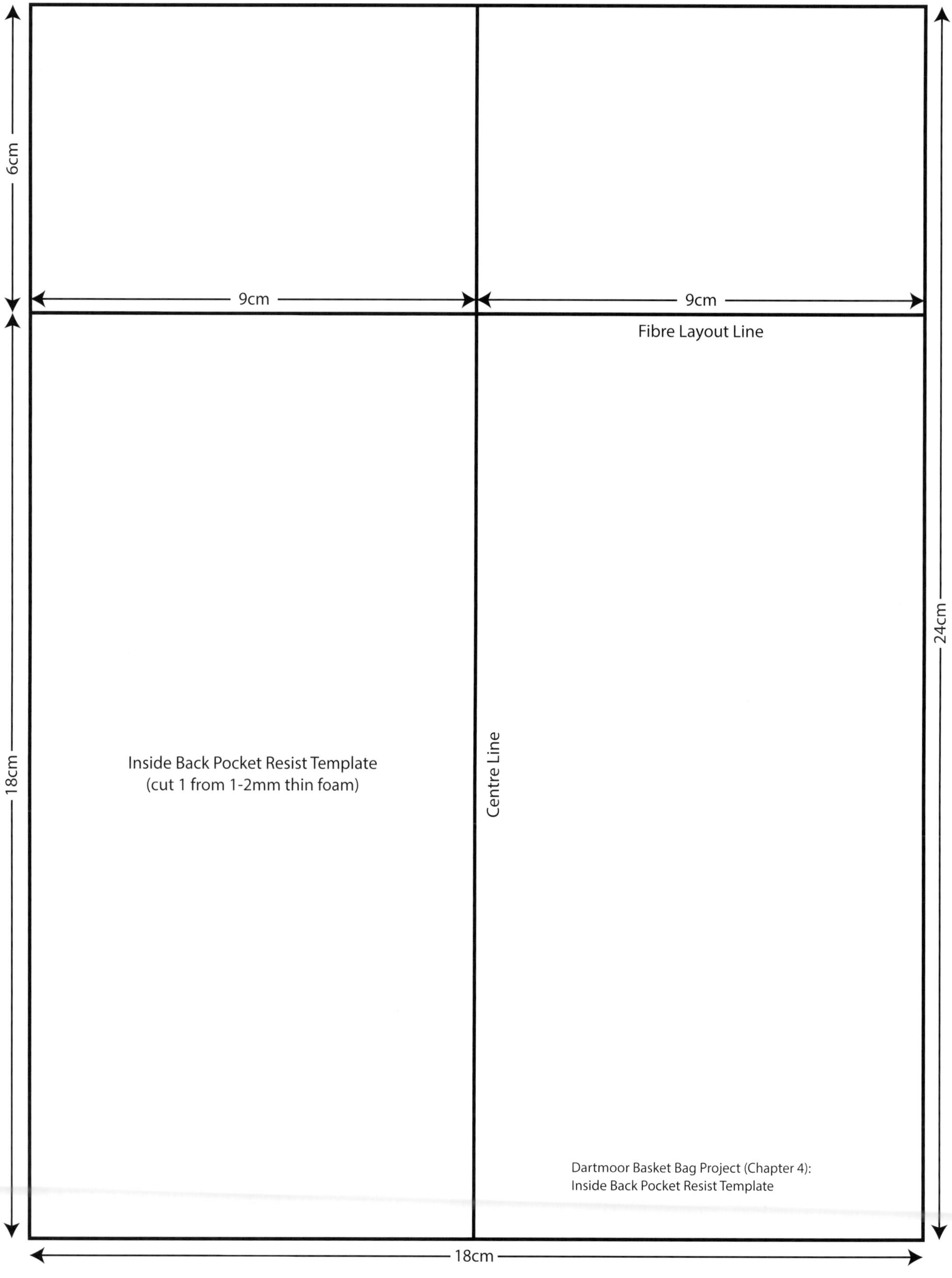
6cm
9cm
9cm
Fibre Layout Line
18cm
24cm
Inside Back Pocket Resist Template
(cut 1 from 1-2mm thin foam)
Centre Line
Dartmoor Basket Bag Project (Chapter 4):
Inside Back Pocket Resist Template
18cm

BACKPACK PROJECT

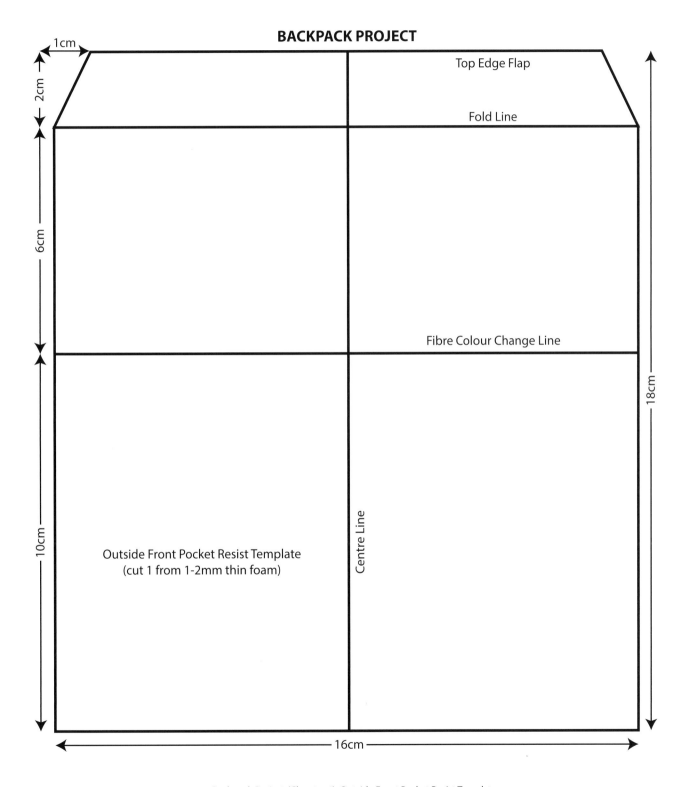

1cm

2cm

6cm

10cm

18cm

16cm

Top Edge Flap

Fold Line

Fibre Colour Change Line

Centre Line

Outside Front Pocket Resist Template
(cut 1 from 1-2mm thin foam)

Backpack Project (Chapter 4): Outside Front Pocket Resist Template

BACKPACK PROJECT

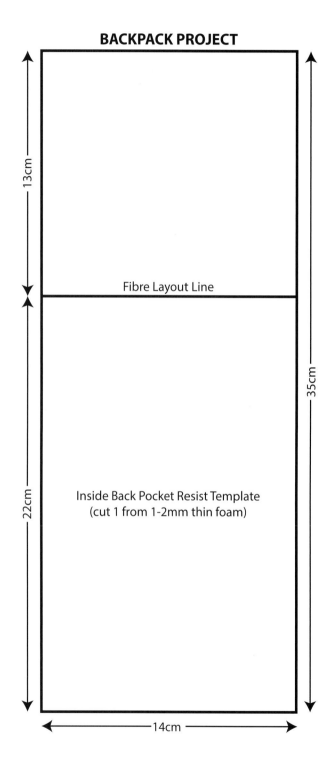

13cm

Fibre Layout Line

35cm

22cm

Inside Back Pocket Resist Template
(cut 1 from 1-2mm thin foam)

14cm

Backpack Project (Chapter 4): Inside Back Pocket Resist Template

CAT CAVE PROJECT

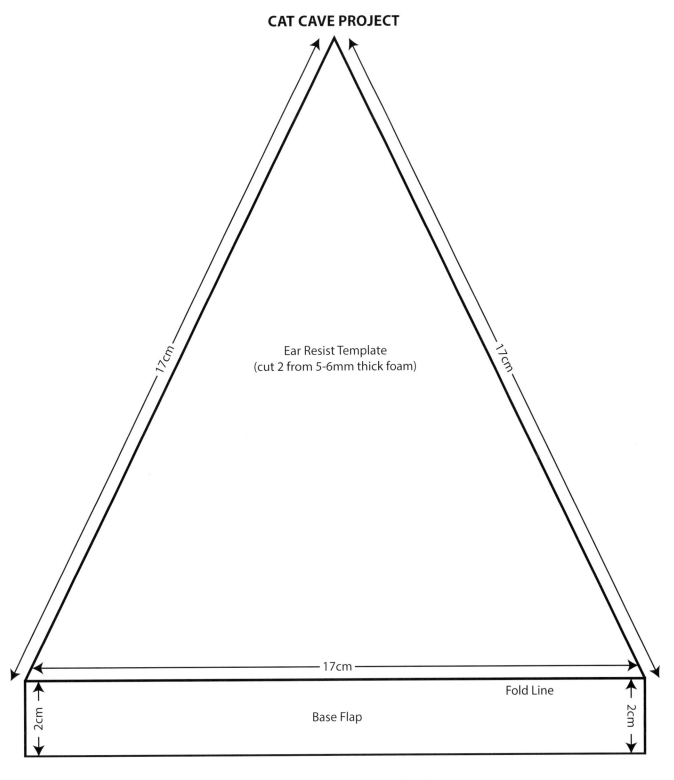

17cm

17cm

Ear Resist Template
(cut 2 from 5-6mm thick foam)

17cm

Fold Line

2cm

Base Flap

2cm

Cat Cave Project (Chapter 4): Ear Resist Template

CONVERSION TABLES

Sizes: Metric to Imperial

Centimetres	Inches (Decimal)	Inches (Fraction)
0.1cm (1mm)	0.04in	$\frac{3}{64}$in
1cm	0.39in	$\frac{25}{64}$in
2cm	0.79in	$\frac{25}{32}$in
3cm	1.18in	1 $\frac{3}{16}$in
4cm	1.57in	1 $\frac{37}{64}$in
5cm	1.97in	1 $\frac{31}{32}$in
6cm	2.36in	2 $\frac{23}{64}$in
7cm	2.76in	2 $\frac{3}{4}$in
8cm	3.15in	3 $\frac{5}{32}$in
9cm	3.54in	3 $\frac{35}{64}$in
10cm	3.94in	3 $\frac{15}{16}$in
20cm	7.87in	7 $\frac{7}{8}$in
30cm	11.81in	11 $\frac{13}{16}$in
40cm	15.78in	15 $\frac{3}{4}$in
50cm	19.69in	19 $\frac{11}{16}$in
60cm	23.62in	23 $\frac{5}{8}$in
70cm	27.56in	27 $\frac{9}{16}$in
80cm	31.5in	31 $\frac{1}{2}$in
90cm	35.43in	35 $\frac{7}{16}$in
100cm (1m)	39.37in	39 $\frac{3}{8}$in

Weight: Grams to Ounces

For simplicity's sake, I've only included weights in grams (g) throughout this book. Below is an approximate conversion table you may find useful if you need to convert grammes to ounces.

Grams	Ounces
1g	0.04oz
2g	0.07oz
3g	0.11oz
4g	0.14oz
5g	0.18oz
6g	0.21oz
7g	0.25oz
8g	0.28oz
9g	0.32oz
10g	0.35oz
20g	0.71oz
30g	1.06oz
40g	1.41oz
50g	1.76oz
60g	2.12oz
70g	2.47oz
80g	2.82oz
90g	3.17oz
100g	3.53oz

Glossary

Wool terminology can be interchangeable (especially between countries), so here is a brief guide to some of the main UK terms as used in this book.

Batt/Batting: fibre (usually wool) that has been cleaned and brushed in a process called carding to create a puffy sheet or 'batt' of fibre, in which the fibres are all laying in different directions. Also synonymous with carded batt and carded fleece.

Book resist: flat, 2D flap-like template around which you add fibre, like the page of a book, to achieve a 3D element.

Carded batt/Carded fleece: *see* batt fibre.

Carded wool: as a general term, wool fibre which has been cleaned and brushed in a process called carding. Also synonymous with batt or batting.

Combed wool: as a general term, wool fibre which has been carded and then combed into long lengths or tubes (called tops), in which the fibres are all lying in one direction.

Felt: a non-woven fabric comprising interlocking wool fibres.

Felting: is a general term for making felt. As a specific term, the felting stage during the wet felting process is when the scales on the fibres lock together and the fibres start to bond to create a very loose fabric (called prefelt).

Felting ball: a type of resist used to create 3D hollow forms.

Fibres: the individual wool (or other material) strands.

Finishing forma: a 3D form used to shape the finished felt and stretch the surface smooth.

Fleece: the unprocessed wool shorn from a sheep.

Fulling: the final stage of the wet felting process when the wool fibres bond together completely and, as they interlock more tightly, the loose prefelt shrinks to create a firm felt fabric.

Laminated felt: *see* nuno felt.

Needle felting: the dry process of bonding fibres together to create felt using a felting needle.

Nuno felt: wool fibre felted into cloth to create a new combined and completely integrated fabric, also known as laminated felt.

Nuno felting: the wet felting process of bonding wool fibre with fabric.

Plant fibre: any fibre originating from a plant, such as viscose or bamboo, and usually processed into tops.

Prefelt/Pre-felt: the term for wool fibres which are partially felted together but have not yet reached the fulling/shrinkage stage. It is available commercially in sheets/fabric, including as thin ribbon strips.

Protein fibre: any fibre originating from an animal, such as wool, mohair or silk.

Resist: a template shape or form made of plastic or another non-feltable material used between wool fibre layers to stop them felting together, to create hollow or pocket-like felted shapes.

Roving: Canadian/US term for a continuous thick cord or strip of batt fibre, *see* sliver.

Shrinkage rate: the percentage decrease in size of the finished felt from its original layout size after wet felting.

Slippage: refers to when the felting ball loosens and moves within the felt shape on the ball during agitation.

Sliver: a continuous flat length or narrow tube of batt fibre. NB: Synonymous with roving in Canada/US.

Top/Tops: fibre (usually wool) that has been processed a stage further than batt fibre to comb it into continuous long, narrow, smooth tube-like lengths, with the shorter hairs removed and all the remaining longer fibres combed neatly in one direction. Other protein and plant fibres can also be processed into tops form.

Wet felting: the general term for the process of applying water, agitation, soap and heat to wool fibre to create felt.

Wool fibre: the general term for processed wool of any kind.

Wool yarn: wool fibre which has been spun into thin, twisted lengths of wool for knitting, crochet or weaving for example.

SUPPLIERS OF FIBRES, EMBELLISHMENT MATERIALS AND WET FELTING EQUIPMENT

UK

Adelaide Walker
Unit 22, Town Head Mills, Main
Street, Addingham,
Ilkley, West Yorkshire, LS29 0PD
www.adelaidewalker.co.uk

Barn2Yarn
Stotfold, Hertfordshire
www.barn2yarnshop.com

Firbeck Fibre Art
Firbeck, South Yorkshire
www.firbeckfibreart.co.uk

Natali Stewart
St. Leonards-on-Sea, East Sussex
www.natalistewart.co.uk

Norwegian Wool
2 New Street, Carnforth, Lanca-
shire, LA5 9BU
www.norwegianwool.co.uk

The Felt Box
Peterborough, Northamptonshire
www.thefeltbox.uk

Wingham Wool Work
Gloucestershire
www.winghamwoolwork.co.uk

World of Wool
Unit 8, The Old Railway Goods Yard,
Scar Lane, Milnsbridge, Huddersfield,
West Yorkshire, HD3 4PE
www.worldofwool.co.uk

Europe

DHG Shop
Prato, Italy
www.dhgshop.it

Piiku
Piesalantilantie 17, 41900 Petäjäv-
esi, Finland
www.piiku.fi

Schapenvacht en Lifestyle
Hoogstraat 32, 962ES Wijk bij
Duurstede, Holland
www.schapenvachtenlifestyle.nl

Wollknoll GmbH
Forsthausstraße 7, 74420, Ober-
rot-Neuhausen, Germany
www.wollknoll.eu

Australia

Fibre Arts Shed
Jilliby, NSW
www.fibreartsshed.com.au

Kraftkolour
Unit 2, 99 Heyington Ave, Thomas-
town, Victoria 3074
www.kraftkolour.net.au

Sally Ridgway Designs
PO Box 683, Quoiba, Tasmania 7310
www.sallyridgway.com.au

Unicorn Fibres
Churchlands, Perth
www.unicornfibres.com.au

Canada

Custom Woolen Mills Ltd
30453 Range Road 27-2, Carstairs,
Alberta T0M 0N0
www.customwoolenmills.com

Legacy Studio
212 West Terrace Point, Cochrane,
Alberta T4C 1S1
www.legacystudio.ca

The Olive Sparrow
19 Waterman Avenue, Suite 202,
Toronto, Ontario M4B 1Y2
www.theolivesparrow.com

SUPPLIERS OF OTHER MATERIALS AND EQUIPMENT

Bag Hardware
www.trimmingshop.co.uk
www.valuebeltsplus.com

Chunky Wool and Mohair Yarn
www.colinetteyarns.com
www.hobbii.co.uk
www.lindehobby.co.uk
www.spectrumfibre.co.uk
www.universalyarn.com

Ethafoam for Templates
www.easyfoam.co.uk

For most of the non-felting-specific materials (such as cushion pads, bag hardware, straps and clasps, sequined fabric) and equipment (such as exercise balls, foam and plastic sheeting, plastic bowls), you will find a big choice online from sites such as Ali Express, Amazon, eBay and Etsy.

FURTHER INFORMATION AND RESOURCES

Books
For an introduction to all aspects of wet felting you might enjoy my first book *Wet Felting* (The Crowood Press Ltd, 2022).

Websites
International Feltmakers Association (IFA)
The International Feltmakers Association is a not-for-profit organisation established to promote felt in all its forms. Membership offers access to a wealth of information and education about all aspects of feltmaking worldwide and includes a quarterly magazine, *Felt Matters*.

www.feltmakers.com

Further information about **Natasha Smart**'s in-person and online wet felting workshops and tutorials is available online.

www.natashasmarttextiles.co.uk.

USA
HeartFelt Silks
243 Third Street, North
Bayport, MN 55003
www.heartfeltsilks.com

Living Felt
2440 E Highway 290, Ste E1, Dripping
Springs, TX 78620
www.feltingsupplies.livingfelt.com
www.feltingtutorials.com

Mohair and More
231 Gibbs Street, Hwy 150, New
Waverly, TX 77358
www.mohairandmore.com

Outback Fibers
PO Box 55, Coaldale, CO 81222
www.outbackfibers.com

Sarafina Fiber Art
1752B Appleton Road,
Elkton, MD 21921
www.sarafinafiberart.com

You will also find lots of independent smaller-scale fibre suppliers based worldwide on Etsy (www.etsy.com) and elsewhere online.

Main Project Guide

Embellished Bowl Sample Project

Coiled Rope Vessel Project

Slouchy Hat Project

Mandala Crochet Cushion Project
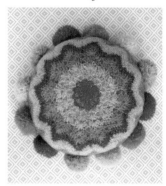

Floral Basket Project

Dartmoor Basket Bag Project

Backpack Project

Cat Cave Project

Sparkle Star Bag Project

Sari Silk Bowl Project

Silk Cowl Project

Jurassic Basket Project

Index

First published in 2024 by
The Crowood Press Ltd
Ramsbury, Marlborough
Wiltshire SN8 2HR

enquiries@crowood.com
www.crowood.com

British Library Cataloguing-in-Publication Data
A catalogue record for this book is available from
the British Library.

ISBN 978 0 7198 4376 1

Cover design by Sergey Tsvetkov

Natasha Smart has asserted her right under the
Copyright, Designs and Patents Act 1988 to be
identified as the author of this work

Typeset by SJmagic DESIGN SERVICES, India.
Printed and bound in India by Parksons Graphics

ACKNOWLEDGEMENTS

I'm incredibly fortunate that through my wet felting obsession I've met so many talented creative people, whether that's other feltmakers, participants on my courses or other textile artists online. I love being a part of this wider textile community where we are all inspiring and learning from each other. So this book is dedicated to everyone out there who enjoys creating with wool fibre, I hope you also find some inspiration in this book.

Thank you to my always supportive family and friends, particularly my parents Melinda and Michael Gane, and my wonderful husband Steve, who have all continued to be massively encouraging. I honestly couldn't have written this book without Steve's sound advice, love and support. And the cats are particularly pleased I finally got around to felting them a cat cave.

Very special thanks to talented photographer Ellie Burgin, who provided the majority of the photographs in this book (except the project step-by-step and progress photos, taken by the author) and has really helped bring my designs and techniques to life. I wouldn't have been able to share the felting on a ball technique without the support of the incredible Marie Spaulding and her team at *Living Felt*, who have been producing felting balls for many years. My fabulous friends Sue Ainsworth and Gill Ladbrook deserve medals for enthusiastically helping me (not just once either) organise the ever-increasing woolly stash in my studio whilst I was creating the designs in this book. And a big thank you to the amazing Sharan Sargeant, who tested several of the projects for me and provided much-appreciated advice and encouragement.

Ellie Burgin Photography, Instagram @ellieburgin2.0
Living Felt, www.feltingsupplies.livingfelt.com